CW01402009

The Inside Careers Guide to Information Technology 2001

Published in association with
the British Computer Society

ⓘ Inside Careers

www.insidecareers.co.uk

Associate member of
**THE ASSOCIATION OF
GRADUATE RECRUITERS**

Contents

The insiders

Education, training & development

Finding the right job

Key recruiters

Publisher
Cambridge Market Intelligence Limited
The Quadrangle
49 Atalanta Street
London SW6 6TR
Telephone 020 7565 7900
Fax 020 7565 7938

Associate Publisher
The British Computer Society
1 Sanford Street
Swindon SN1 1HJ
Telephone 01793 417417
Fax 01793 480270

We are indebted to the British
Computer Society for its support, in
particular to Aline Cumming and Colin
Thompson for their help and guidance
throughout the preparation of the *Guide*
and for reviewing the text for balance
and accuracy.

Managing Editor Richard Green
Production Editor Jayne Hale

Advertising enquiries
Telephone 020 7565 7900
Fax 020 7565 7938
E-mail sales@cmi.co.uk

This compilation © 2000
Cambridge Market Intelligence Limited

Copyright in individual articles © 2000
the authors, who have asserted their
right to be identified as the author under
s.78 of the Copyright, Designs and
Patents Act 1988.

ISBN 1 86213 056 6

Printed and bound in Spain by
Grafo S.A., Ariz-Basauri (Vizcaya)

Foreword

I am delighted that you can join me in exploring a career in IT – the computers that organise information and the communications that make it available to us. Whether you are buying books on the World Wide Web or are developing a career in weather forecasting, you are benefiting from the many swift changes in technology which are making the world more exciting every day. Happily, we cannot today even begin to forecast the limits of those changes.

We therefore need a force of IT professionals with technical competence, flexibility and, above all, imagination – who can understand the business or the academic or the public sector environments in which new IT systems will be working – and who will play their part in developing them. IT professionals work to high standards to produce quality products to a deadline, particularly in areas where safety and security are concerned.

Remember the benefits of joining a professional body. You will be able to keep in touch with the frequent, and inevitable, changes in practice taking place in the IT industry – and play your part in making sure that they happen. Membership will also enable you to keep your own professional development under review and, hopefully, help your own career development.

I wish you well in your chosen career. If you decide to follow a career in this fascinating business, you will find challenges and occasional frustrations; but it will be satisfying and, I trust, financially rewarding.

Enjoy!

Alastair Macdonald
President-elect, British Computer Society

the industry

What are IT and information systems?

IT and information systems

No invention has transformed our world so comprehensively as the computer. It is just over 50 years since the successful running of the world's first stored-program computer at Manchester University. From that pioneering work have flowed computer applications that touch all our lives every minute of every day.

The scale of the achievement comes from the ability to integrate computer technology with communications technology which, together, as information technology (IT), can deliver information almost instantaneously around the globe.

No other technology has advanced so fast. Every year new advances make possible information systems that were previously impractical. Building the vast systems that run on today's computers is an engineering activity that stands comparison with the greatest achievements of the nineteenth-century engineers who transformed that society. Modern information systems are now the most complex artefacts yet made by human beings.

Scope of IT

Nothing for me illustrates the power of IT as well as the airline industry which so many of us have come to take for granted. Our trips usually start with a visit to a travel agent. In the past the travel agent used a vast paper-based timetable and a telephone to book a seat. Today an online computer terminal gives details of flights and can then make a booking. A credit card payment with online authorisation

Roger Johnson

Roger Johnson is President of the Council of European Professional Informatics Societies (CEPIS), and a Past President of the British Computer Society (BCS). He began his career writing software for major financial institutions and, since becoming an academic, has taught information systems design and data management. He is currently Dean of the Faculty of Social Science and Reader in Computer Science at Birkbeck College, London University.

ensures we can walk away with our tickets.

When we check in, computer workstations allocate us seats. While we are arriving the aircrew are agreeing their flight plans with Air Traffic Control, the aircraft is refuelled and the provisions for the flight are loaded, with details of the passengers' seats for special meals, all managed by a series of information systems.

When we board the aircraft we enter another world, where information systems rule. Increasingly for much of the flight the pilots do not fly the aircraft but monitor its behaviour against their preset flight plan.

Yet in the past couple of years airlines have been able to make further major advances. Minor faults detected by onboard systems on the previous flight and notified automatically to the destination can be quickly fixed so that aircraft can depart on schedule for their next

flight. Aircraft such as the A320 have replaced many of the mechanical control systems with digital systems. Travel agents face a challenge to their future as leading airlines offer online ticket booking over the Internet and, more recently, electronic ticketing, which does away with conventional tickets altogether.

One of the most remarkable aspects of this whole revolution is that the computer systems, apart from at the travel agent and at check in, are largely invisible to the passengers and yet without them mass commercial air transport would be impossible. Everywhere around us, at home with the telephone, car and domestic appliances, travelling to work by train and traffic control, and at work with all kinds of applications our lives are affected by information systems. In every case we barely notice their presence. Consequently I have often referred in articles to information systems engineers as 'invisible engineers'.

The information society

Starting from nowhere in the early 1990s, the Internet is revolutionising the availability of information of all sorts. No major company can be without its Web site. Increasingly companies are advancing from just giving information to developing electronic commerce – selling their products over the Internet. Furthermore, once the information is on the Web, it is available worldwide. When I travel to northern Europe by train I prefer the

German railway Web site, because it gives a near universal coverage of European train services, unlike the British service. Whenever possible, I also buy my ticket from them as well.

German railway Web site

In future most paper-based reference material will become available online. However, today's static paper images will soon be replaced by images with all the benfits of multimedia. This will represent the ultimate extension of the Internet into a public information utility. However, this introduces a crucial issue about designing and maintaining public information systems. The professionals who build and maintain such systems have a special responsibility of care in their construction. Like many other engineers, information systems engineers derive satisfaction from seeing others using the artefacts they have built. However, without understating the complexity of building a bridge, an information system is a much more complex artefact. In particular, the interaction between it and its user is far more complex.

Early computerised information systems often had several layers of employ-

> "...information systems engineers derive satisfaction from seeing others using the artefacts they have built."

ees between the customer and the computer. The modern system, such as one on the Internet, however, has no such intermediaries to check its output. Erroneous data supplied to Internet users may cause serious inconvenience. I have found mistakes in both airline and rail timetable systems. Although this is easily corrected, I could have gone to the wrong airport or waited for a non-existent train.

Professionalism

Information systems professionals carry heavy responsibilities on their shoulders. This is why a career in information systems can be rewarding. But it is not to be undertaken lightly. Many people today can carry out useful calculations with a spreadsheet or create simple database systems. However, the test of the true information systems professional is whether they would trust their own well-being and, ultimately, their lives to their own programming. Would you fly in an aircraft that was using software you had written?

In the run-up to 1 January 2000, organisations spent huge amounts of money ensuring that their software would continue to operate correctly in the new millennium. As a result, although many organisations experienced minor faults, none of the more extravagant prophesies were fulfilled. However, no citizen can have been left in any doubt about society's total dependence on information systems and the individuals who create and operate them. The next big challenge is the politicians' decision to move to the new euro currency. This decision is causing information systems not only across Europe but right round the world to be rewritten to an externally decided timetable.

These two challenges demonstrate another key attribute of information systems: information systems evolve. There are always changes to be made and facilities updated. Every significant development in an organisation must necessarily br preceded by the modification of the information systems. Such is our collective dependence on information systems and the professionals behind them.

Information systems are at the heart of every developed society. They are essential to the standard of living we have all come to expect. Only properly trained professionals can ensure that the world has the information systems it needs to ensure the well-being of every citizen.

History and development of IT

In 1834 Babbage invented the first computer, which he called the Analytical Engine, but he never completed it. Unfortunately for Babbage, he was handicapped by the costly mechanical technology of his day and it would be a century before such machines were both technologically and economically feasible. Until then information processing had to be achieved by simpler methods.

Before the computer

Large-scale information processing took off in the 1850s with the development of mass markets for information goods and services, such as life insurance, bank accounts and cheap telegrams. In order to satisfy these markets huge offices were established in London and the provinces, where hundreds or sometimes thousands of clerks beavered away performing tasks that would now be done by a computer. These clerks – often youngsters fresh from elementary school – spent long working days hunched over a desk transcribing documents in long-hand or processing bank accounts without the aid of a calculating machine.

In the 1880s and 1890s the work of office clerks was transformed by the

Martin Campbell-Kelly

Martin Campbell-Kelly is Reader in Computer Science at the University of Warwick. He has lectured and written widely on the history of computing. His publications include the official history of ICL, Britain's leading information systems firm, and the collected works of Charles Babbage.

development of office machines such as typewriters and adding machines. Much of this development took place in the United States, and several major firms, such as Remington Typewriter and the Burroughs Adding Machine Company, later became leading suppliers of computers. Another major office-machine firm was International Business Machines (IBM), which started out in 1896 producing punched-card machines which automatically processed data recorded as holes punched on manila cards. The ancestor of Britain's ICL was also established at the turn of the century as a manufacturer of punched-card equipment.

Invention of the computer

The first electronic computers were

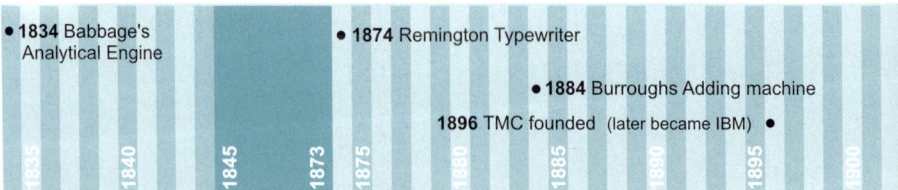

- **1834** Babbage's Analytical Engine
- **1874** Remington Typewriter
- **1884** Burroughs Adding machine
- **1896** TMC founded (later became IBM)

1835 1840 1845 1873 1875 1880 1885 1890 1895 1900

invented as a response to the need for computer power during the Second World War. In Britain, for example, the mathematician Alan Turing was one of the minds behind the Colossus computer, developed in top secret at Bletchley Park to break the codes of the German High Command, which played a decisive part in the Allied victory.

The most spectacular wartime computer development was the mammoth ENIAC built at the University of Pennsylvania, designed by two young researchers, John Presper Eckert and John Mauchly. Even before the ENIAC was completed, however, it was seen to have serious design flaws – not the least of which was that it contained 18,000 electronic tubes that consumed 150 kilowatts of electric power. In 1945, Eckert and Mauchly were joined by the world-famous mathematician John von Neumann and others, and between them they established a new computer design – now often known as the von Neumann architecture. This is the design on which almost all of today's computers are based.

Electronic data processing
In 1955 there were just 263 computers in the world. These were mostly used for scientific calculations in research laboratories and universities. However, a few visionaries saw very early on that the computer also had a potential for office work. In America, Eckert and Mauchly obtained finance to build a data processing computer known as UNIVAC, and thus laid the foundations of the present Unisys Corporation.

Similarly, in Britain, a group of office managers in the catering firm of J Lyons decided to build a computer called LEO – for Lyons Electronic Office – and later established a computer manufacturing organisation, Leo Computers Limited. This firm was later one of those that combined in the 1960s to form the present ICL.

The DEUCE – a popular British computer of the 1950s

By the mid-1950s, most of the old-line office-machine firms, such as IBM, Burroughs, NCR and Remington Rand, had responded to the new opportunity for electronic data processing and had transformed their electro-mechanical products into electronic computers. The 'mainframe' computers of the 1950s were very large, and even a medium-sized installation cost the equivalent of £1m in today's money. Because they were built using electronic-tube technology they

- **1907** BTM founded (later became ICL)
- **1937** Turing Machine theoretical computer
- **1943** Colossus code-breaking machine •
- **1945** ENIAC computer •
- **1945** Von Neuman's EDVAC Report •

1905　1910　1915　1935　1940　1945

were slow, and produced so much heat that they could only be operated in air-conditioned rooms with forced cooling. By 1960 there were about 6,000 computers installed worldwide.

The revolution in electronics
In the late 1950s electronic tubes began to be replaced by discrete transistors. The new technology transformed the computer, improving its speed and reliability by an order of magnitude, as well as producing far less heat. Computers also became much cheaper. For the first time electronic data processing computers became practical for ordinary, medium-sized businesses and they were sold in tens of thousands. By the mid-1960s there were about 30,000 computers in the world.

The next evolutionary stage in the development of electronics was integrated circuits, in which a single 'chip' contained the equivalent of a dozen or more transistors. Integrated circuits produced another leap in computer speed and reliability, and a further reduction in cost. The result was not only more powerful mainframe computers, but also small business computers that were ideal for small and medium-sized firms. Other small machines – dubbed minicomputers – were developed for process control, road traffic management, and many other areas where previously the cost of a mainframe computer would have been prohibitive. By the mid-1970s there were more than a quarter of a million computers in operation around the world.

Real-time applications
The first computer applications were not very imaginative, but simply replaced old-fashioned electromechanical technology with electronics, without changing the underlying information system. Thus ordinary people were often unaffected by computers – a bank statement looked very much the same whether it was produced by a punched-card machine or a computer.

In the 1960s, however, a revolutionary change in business operations occurred when computers were used to perform data processing in real time, so that the information system could react almost instantly to events in the real world. The first real-time applications in the 1960s were for airline reservation systems, and by the 1970s most of the major banks had installed real-time automatic teller machines.

The software for these major business applications often consisted of a million lines or more of code, whose development required a small army of analysts and programmers. In the largest firms – such as insurance companies and banks – data processing departments with a hundred or more staff were established to create these information systems, and many of these firms remain major recruiters of computing graduates. Other firms, however, lacked the expertise to develop complex information systems, so that management consultancies and software-writing firms came into existence to satisfy this demand. Today's major computer-serv-

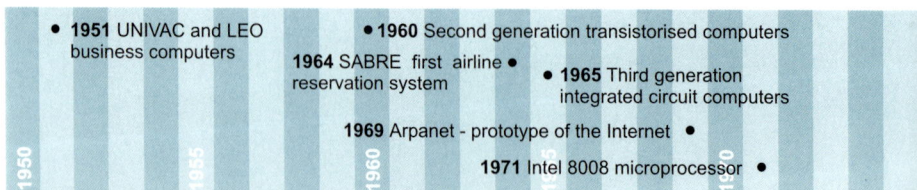

- **1951** UNIVAC and LEO business computers
- **1960** Second generation transistorised computers
- **1964** SABRE first airline reservation system
- **1965** Third generation integrated circuit computers
- **1969** Arpanet - prototype of the Internet
- **1971** Intel 8008 microprocessor

1950　1955　1960　1965　1970

ices organisations and software houses, most of which were established in the 1960s and 1970s, are key employers of computing graduates.

The personal computer

The electronics revolution has continued without pause since the mid-1960s, with the number of active components on a chip doubling roughly every 18 months – a phenomenon known as Moore's Law (named after Gordon Moore, a founder of the Intel Corporation). In 1971 Intel produced the first 'microprocessor' – a complete computer processor on a single chip. Although only a quarter of an inch square, that microprocessor was at least as powerful as the 30-ton ENIAC of 1945. Today's microprocessors are hundreds of times more powerful again.

At first, microprocessors found a market in electronic games and automobile electronics. But soon computer amateurs and technical hobbyists took to the microprocessor, and produced the first personal computers. In 1977, firms such as Apple, Tandy and Commodore began to produce personal computers for non-technical people – initially targeted at home and educational users. In Britain, firms such as Sinclair and Amstrad also helped establish the market for personal computers.

By about 1980, with the development of software such as wordprocessors and spreadsheets, the personal computer began to find a role in the office. In 1981, IBM fully legitimated the new style of computing by producing its first 'PC'.

Over the next decade the IBM PC and compatible machines from other manufacturers transformed the working environment of most office workers and changed many aspects of computer usage. Today there are probably more than 500 million personal computers in use around the world, and the firms that supply them became some of the fastest-growing business operations of the twentieth century.

The Internet

In the 1990s the new frontier of computing moved on from the isolated personal computer to the world of networked computers. Although the basic technology of the Internet was established in the 1970s for use in universities and research laboratories, the expanding capabilities of the personal computer in the early 1990s caused the Internet to grow exponentially. Whereas in 1990 there had been just a quarter of a million computers linked to the Internet, in 1995 the number exceeded 6 million. By 2000 there were 72 million.

All over the world, existing businesses are using the Internet for the marketing of goods and services – known as e-commerce, and to enable their employees to collaborate more effectively. At the same time, many new firms are springing up offering software to access and locate information on the Internet, and others are planning to provide information on goods and services as yet undreamed of.

Today's computing practitioner has the opportunity to help shape that future.

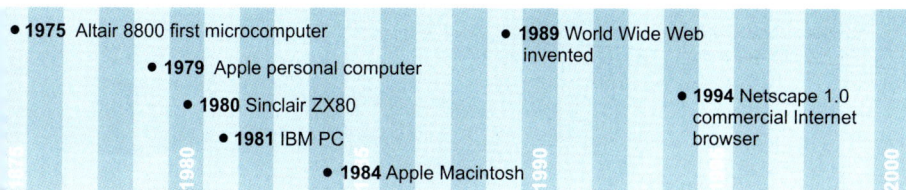

- **1975** Altair 8800 first microcomputer
- **1979** Apple personal computer
- **1980** Sinclair ZX80
- **1981** IBM PC
- **1984** Apple Macintosh
- **1989** World Wide Web invented
- **1994** Netscape 1.0 commercial Internet browser

1980

1990

2000

Organisation of the industry

The information systems industry represents one of the most dynamic and important parts of the economy. Today every aspect of life uses computing in some way or another and the explosion of electronic business is opening huge new opportunities.

The role of the industry is to supply the products and services that allow user organisations (including IT producers!) to make full use of the potential of technology. Products take many forms – computers, packaged software, consultancy, computing services, and this applies whether the business is the latest .com company or a traditional manufacturer of computing equipment.

The industry has several major sectors: computing services, product suppliers and system integrators. Companies vary in size from the giant multinational companies such as Microsoft to the small innovative companies specialising in a

Judith Scott

Judith Scott is the Secretary General and Chief Executive of the British Computer Society.

specific application. There are opportunities for those interested in starting their own company and those interested in highly complex high-investment developments.

Computing services

Computing services are very diverse. Modern Internet service providers are most frequently in the public eye as they are usually the initial point of contact with the Internet for ordinary members of the public. These businesses offer basic connectivity services to the Internet, and basic Web presence for small users. Web-based Internet services include development of Web sites, Internet facilities for

IT practitioners and users in IT supplier and user organisations in the UK (1998)

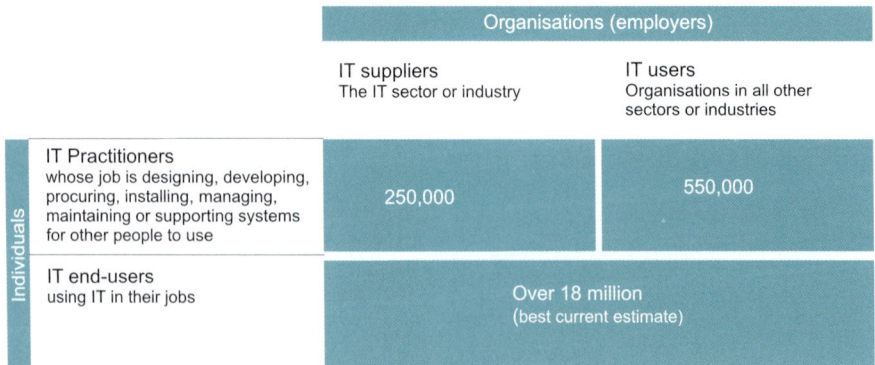

	Organisations (employers)	
	IT suppliers The IT sector or industry	IT users Organisations in all other sectors or industries
IT Practitioners whose job is designing, developing, procuring, installing, managing, maintaining or supporting systems for other people to use	250,000	550,000
IT end-users using IT in their jobs	Over 18 million (best current estimate)	

(left side label: Individuals)

electronic commerce and specialist networks for communities such as schools. Companies offering the more complex services often include the sophisticated use of Internet technology with the design flair needed to present information effectively. Companies offering Web services vary from small start-up companies to specialist sections of large multinational consultants organisations. New business are being created every day, and there is a rapidly growing demand for skills in this area offering many exciting opportunities to innovate.

Despite all the excitement of the new opportunities in the Internet, there is still a need to keep the behind-the-scenes operations running effectively in support of the business, and e-business systems need to interconnect with core systems if the business is to benefit fully from the new facilities. This ongoing services business provides advice and support to businesses on their total IT strategy, and sometimes provides the full computing support structure for an organisation. Computer services of this type can offer a wonderful opportunity to work with a large variety of organisations on many different applications of technology. They can be organisations which specify systems for users and project manage the implementation; or Internet companies providing the infrastructure for e-business; or the outsourcing companies operating computing activities for user organisations. Many user companies whose primary business is not computing maintain a substantial IT function to support their business activities.

Product suppliers

Product suppliers design and produce technology which others employ. Like many other industries, there are specialist component suppliers, whose products are consumed by higher-level producers. Others produce kits from which specific systems can be built by other professionals or skilled users and there are products complete and ready for use.

Components in the IT sector can be either software or hardware. They are technically well defined, and address a narrow area in depth. People working in this field are highly skilled specialists, and are often involved with technical standards.

Hardware suppliers

Hardware comes from a variety of organisations. Traditional large mainframe manufacurers continue to supply high-volume high-performance equipment for commercial core application servers and large repositories of data. PC manufacturers supply ever increasingly capable workstation equipment which provides the backbone of the home use PC market and the desktop usage in most businesses. And network equipment companies provide the products that interconnect workstations and computer systems.

There is also a supplier community in microprocessors, concerned with the integration of microprocessors into a variety of devices, including PCs. A huge variety of modern electrical devices have embedded microprocessors, from the microwave oven in the kitchen to the energy management systems on modern cars. The variety is limited only by the capacity of human innovation.

Another key part of the hardware product sector is the provision of expanding ranges of new peripherals for computers. The range is growing rapidly, from new forms of scanners and digital cameras, multimedia and CD-ROMs to robotics. These are often developed by small innovative companies whose staff are at the leading edge of research coming out of the universities.

Generic software

This is the software that makes computers easy to use but does not tailor them for any specific business purpose. It includes packages such as Windows, and the suites of packages for wordprocessing, spread-sheets and databases. A variety of software specialists and hardware manufacturers develop software on which to build specific applications. There is a general acceptance of the need for 'open systems', so that applications developed on one computer can be operated on those from different manufacturers using the same platform. Generic software includes not only the core operating systems, but also data architecture and management systems, complex networking software and desktop management tools. It also provides the basis of the software tools for the Internet and the World Wide Web, which are the new areas of investment for generic software, including middleware which bridges between traditional back office systems and Web-based applications. Exciting new areas of generic software include software robots and intelligent agents, both of which provide customised access to the information on the Web for individuals.

This kind of software is often complex, and companies with large financial resources normally undertake development. Projects can take years to complete and test, and provide developers with detailed experience in information systems.

One area of continuing innovation lies in image manipulation. Advances in image-enhancing techniques have had a big impact on the space programme. The defects in the Hubble telescope mirror were repaired in part by the use of image-enhancing software, and the pictures we now receive are of startling clarity, despite the flaws in the mirror and the distortion produced in sending the data back to earth.

Similarly medicine has had to deal with very poor-quality images from devices such as X-ray machines and body scanning equipment. Initially, computers were used to enhance the image for use by medical professionals. Increasingly the technology is used to identify specific objects and, when combined with robotics, to form entirely new tools for use by medical staff.

Specialist software

A variety of companies large and small produce software for specific business needs. Large systems developments are often concentrated in key industries such as defence, telecommunications and banking, which require very high levels of reliability; professionals working in this area are experts in building failsafe systems. For example, today's modern telephone exchange has many millions of lines of code, which must handle unexpected conditions but not interrupt the service.

The design and implementation of large complex systems are usually undertaken by larger companies, whereas many smaller companies work on smaller applications, ranging from patient management systems for GPs' offices to software for theatrical management. A modern West End theatre set uses information systems for everything from box office bookings to lighting and scene changes.

The film industry is making use of information systems which extend the possibilities for special effects; this may call for image manipulation or creating virtual sets and integrating live film. The computer games industry in the UK is world class, and offers exciting employment opportunities for those with a bent for high-performance computer graphics and an artistic flair.

The key to successful specialist systems is their fit with the business they are designed for. A good general ledger system is just as rewarding as jazzy CD-ROM-based software for the rock music industry. Because of the variety of uses, specialist software offers by far the greatest diversity of areas of work. This sector of the market is constantly evolving. It is exciting, challenging, never dull, and the basis of many successful start-up businesses. Britain has a real strength in software development.

Systems integrators

Large information system projects often require a unique integration of a variety of products and facilities in order to achieve the business objective. Many of today's products are sufficiently easy to install and use that the users do this themselves, but complex systems require many more skills than a single-user organisation can afford to employ, and there are companies specialising in specifying, acquiring, integrating and installing complex systems. Companies offering these services are usually large, and employ people who enjoy the challenge of project management, as well as the detailed work of software development.

Summary

The information systems industry has a huge variety of participants. It offers opportunities to people interested in the depths of technology or in the creative use of new media. It has a place for those wanting to work for large or small companies, or to form their own start-up. You can work in close cooperation with any number of other disciplines, or you can specialise in one, or develop generic approaches. It is wealth creating, growing, innovative and, above all, fun.

Entering the IT maze

Looking at the structure of a career path in IT is rather like looking at a maze. What is more, it is a virtual maze with flexible walls, which are constantly moving, changing and expanding. A dead-end this year may, say with training, be next year's opportunity; an apparent opening may be overtaken by developments and become a dead-end in career terms.

It was already evident back in 1986 that the same job in different sectors of the industry, and even in different sectors of the same company, carries various job titles and varying levels of responsibility. For example, what one organisation calls a programmer another will call a software engineer and what one company sees as a backroom job another will see as customer facing. The British Computer Society and the computing industry collaborated to produce a model of employment in the computing industry, to be used to monitor professional development. When release 3 of the Industry Structure Model (ISM) was planned in 1994 it was clear that a job-based ISM was no longer possible. The technology had moved on and diversified, and downsizing and delayering had destroyed any generally accepted notion of what was and what was not a job or career path. It was eventually agreed to base the ISM on the role, which is defined as the performance of a particular function at a particular level of development. A function is a distinct area of IS activity. The functions are collected into groupings, as shown in Table 1.

Sheelagh Flowerday

Sheelagh Flowerday is a member of the British Computer Society and a Chartered Engineer. As an independent consultant she undertakes work for the British Computer Society and, as a professional development consultant, assists organisations in developing their staff to gain professional status.

The ISM itself describes for each role the competencies and qualifications required, and any training needed for career development. Some 70 functions are included and eight levels of responsibility. Although not all roles will be performed at each level, nevertheless the full ISM is a formidable document, too much to reproduce here. However, we can derive information about certain roles.

Who does what?

We can start by considering functions in three of the groupings, systems development, service delivery and change configuration, and mention some other significant roles.

1. Systems development

The head of a modern systems development department is likely to tell you that the jobs fall into three main areas: software engineering, business analysis and project management.

Software engineers cover the full spectrum of a development life-cycle from definition and design to construction, testing, installation and modification. This seems to imply that the software engineer as a one-man band has effectively replaced the analyst, systems designer and programmer, but in real terms it is a reflection on the way that the majority of organisations work today. Instead of having X programmers, Y systems designers and Z analysts, it makes more sense to have X+Y+Z software engineers, thus reducing the chance of X, Y or Z sitting around waiting on the other two.

Business analysts are primarily concerned with understanding how the business works and translating that understanding into clearly defined and realistic specifications. The requirement specification reflects the business analyst's understanding of the business' requirements and must be agreed with the business before the design specification may be produced. Business analysts may be IT practitioners or from the business itself.

Project managers. The vast majority of IT is bundled up into projects and programmes (the management of a set of related projects that together satisfy a business objective). This makes project management a key role. The project manager is responsible for delivering the project within given time and financial constraints and at the appropriate level of quality. Planning, monitoring progress and initiating corrective action to keep a project on track will necessarily play a large part in the role. Most companies would expect a project manager to have a comprehensive knowledge of the relevant life-cycle of the computer system; this might be from a business or an IT perspective.

2. Service delivery

Within the service delivery area the prime driver is maintaining an efficient IT service in terms of software and hardware networked across one or more sites. The emphasis is on support, planning and control rather than development. As within any working environment, things are likely to go wrong, so a skilled support team is essential to ensure that the IT department meets the needs of the business. A helpdesk will log incidents and enquiries and initiate corrective action by contacting the appropriate team to deal with the problem. These teams are likely to be called:

- User Support, who will respond to breakdowns in the provision of the IT service, usually relating to hardware or equipment;
- Network Support who deal with breakdowns in service across the network; or
- Applications Support, who provide support to both development and service delivery specifically relating to failures in the application systems themselves.

All of these areas also have a day-to-day role in monitoring the system, reporting trends and recommending (corrective) actions as well as dealing with routine maintenance and the day-to-day running of their own area. A large number of organisations have service partners who provide a specific service under contract, such as a helpdesk or network support area. These organisations need a specialist(s) to draw up contracts, and to negotiate with and monitor the effectiveness of such third-party suppliers. Depending upon the size of the organisation, service level monitoring and management (internal as well as third party) and contract monitoring and management may or may not be roles within their own right, but none the less they are an important part of the service delivery and support areas.

3. Change management and configuration management

As you might expect, with a living environment there are frequent updates and changes required to the systems and infrastructure. All these changes need to go through a control procedure to ensure they are introduced into the live systems in such a way as to ensure that service is not interrupted. This is the remit of the change management area. In a similar way the configuration management area is responsible for minimising the impact of a change to the configuration items, for example the introduction of new hardware. Change and configuration management are closely linked and in a number of organisations will be the responsibility of one manager.

As in development, the work in the service delivery area is also bundled up into projects and programmes, hence the role of project manager is one that is common to both development and service delivery. To some extent this also applies to software engineering which encompasses the life-cycle of a project from initiation to implementation. Here the area of application, for example the design, build, test and implementation phases for a credit system versus the design, build, test and implementation phases of an intranet service, spells out the differences.

4. Other significant roles

Outside development and service delivery exist a number of equally important roles such as those involved in quality management and standards, education and training, research, software testing and database design. It is possible to enter these and other specialist areas as a graduate trainee; however, doing so will reduce your options and I would advise you to get good foundation training and experience in systems development or service delivery (or both) before specialising.

A career path?

A lot of people take their first job in IT not knowing what to expect. Given the nature of the IT maze this is not surprising.

While it is a good idea to set yourself goals of the 'Where do you see yourself in five years' time?' variety, they should not be set in concrete. Inevitably as you gain more knowledge your focus may change. You will find that by adopting a flexible and outward-looking approach you will do both yourself and your employer a favour. The modern IT organisation will welcome the graduate who is willing to gain skills across a wide spectrum of IT activities, but be careful to make sure you achieve a balance – avoid gaining too much breadth with little or no depth or vice versa.

To some extent the traditional paths from programmer to analyst to project manager or helpdesk to PC support to networks still exist if you want to follow them, but in the drive to create a skilled, flexible workforce the clear-cut career path is starting to lose its relevance. As most organisations recognise a technical stream there is no obvious reason for a technical specialist to move into a human resource management role to gain promotion. At a senior level, however, he or she would be expected to provide leadership in a wide variety of situations. This is a skill that is common to both the human resource manager and the technical specialist. For example, a senior software engineer or a network analyst might also be a project manager for one or more stages of a project's life-cycle.

Whatever your chosen direction, it is important to ensure that you achieve a good balance between breadth and depth of experience. You should always look behind a job title to find out just what you will be doing.

There's only one thing left to say – good luck!

A more detailed description of the roles mentioned above may be found in the BCS' Industry Structure Model. Please refer to the BCS Web site: WWW.bcs.org.uk for details

Table 1 Roles from ISM Release 3.2

Groupings	Function	Code	Level of responsibility where roles available								
Management	Education and Training Management	ETMG							6	7	8
	Information Resource Management	IRMG							6	7	8
	IS Co-ordination	ISCO							6	7	8/9
	IS Management	ISMG						5	6	7	8/9
	Programme Management	PGMG							6	7	8
	Project Management	PRMG					4	5	6	7	8
	Service Delivery Management	SDMG							6	7	8
	Systems Development Management	DLMG							6	7	8
	Telecommunications Management	TLMG						5	6	7	8
Policy, Planning and Research	Business Continuity Planning	COPL				3	4	5			
	Emerging Technology Monitoring	EMRG						5	6	7	
	IS Strategy and Planning	STPL						5	6	7	
	Network Planning	NTPL						5	6	7	
	Research	RSCH			2	3	4	5	6	7	
Systems Development and Maintenance	Applications Support	ASUP		1	2	3	4				
	Business Analysis	ANAL			2	3	4	5	6	7	
	Data Analysis	DTAN		1	2	3	4	5			
	Database Design	DBDS		1	2	3	4	5	6		
	Documentation/Technical Authoring	DOCM		1	2	3	4	5	6		
	Porting/Software Integration	PORT			2	3	4	5	6		
	Programming/Software Creation	PROG		1	2	3	4				
	Software Engineering	SENG		1	2	3	4	5	6		
	Systems Architecture	ARCH						5	6	7	
	Systems Design	DESN			2	3	4	5	6		
	Systems Integration	SINT		1	2	3					
	Software Testing	TEST		1	2	3	4	5	6	7	
	Web Specialism	WBSP		1	2	3	4	5			
Service Delivery	Capacity Management	CPMG				3	4	5	6		
	Computer Operations	COPS	0	1	2	3	4				
	Database Administration	DBAD		1	2	3	4	5			
	Hardware/Software Installation	HSIN		1	2	3					
	Help Desk	HELP	0	1	2	3	4				
	Network Administration and Support	NTAS			2	3					
	Network Control	NTCO					4	5	6		
	Problem Management	PBMG					4	5			
	Service Delivery Planning and Control	SDPC				3	4	5	6		
	Service Level Monitoring	SLMO			2	3	4	5			
	Systems Programming	SYSP				3	4				
	User Support	USUP		1	2	3	4	5			
Technical Advice and Consultancy	Business Process (Re-)Engineering	BPRE						5	6	7	
	Consultancy	CNSL						5	6	7	8
	Safety Assessment	SFAS						5	6	7	
	Security Specialism	SCTY				3	4	5	6	7	
	Software Process Improvement	SPIM						5	6	7	8
	System Ergonomics Evaluation	HCEV			2	3	4	5	6		

Groupings	Function	Code	Level of responsibility where roles available							
			1	2	3	4	5	6	7	8
	Technical Specialism	TECH				4	5	6		
Quality	IS Audit	AUDT			3	4	5	6	7	8
	Quality Assurance	QUAS				4	5	6		
	Quality Audit	QUAU						6	7	8
	Quality Management	QUMG				4	5	6	7	
	Quality Standards	QUST	1	2	3	4				
Customer Relations	Account Management	ACMG				4	5	6	7	
	Marketing	MKTG		2	3	4	5	6	7	
	Sales Support	SSUP	1	2	3	4	5			
	Selling	SALE			3	4	5	6		
Education and Training	Development and Training	DVTR				4	5	6	7	
	Education and Training Delivery	ETDL		2	3	4	5			
	Training Materials Creation	TMCR				4	5	6	7	
Support and Administration	Appraisal and Assessment	APAS				4	5	6		
	Change Management	CHMG		2	3	4	5	6		
	Configuration Management	CFMG		2	3	4	5	6		
	Contract Management	COMG					5	6	7	
	Contract Monitoring	COMO			3	4	5	6	7	
	Data Protection	DPRO				4	5	6		
	IS Asset Management	ASMG				4	5	6		
	Methods and Tools	METL			3	4	5	6		
	PDS Supervision	SUPV				4				
	Procurement	PROC					5	6	7	
	Project Office	PROF		2	3	4	5			
	Recruitment and Resourcing	RERE				4	5	6	7	
	Security Administration	SCAD		2	3	4				
	Technical Authority	TAUT					5	6	7	

The Internet

The Internet is probably the biggest advance in the use of technology since the advent of the computer. It has created a mass communication and information resource across the world that is easy and inexpensive to use and effective in commercial, social and personal environments.

The Internet has now become mainstream and has spawned the need for an an entirely new range of skills and knowledge. However, it is also important to realise that, essentially, the Internet itself is not a new technology. It uses well-established systems, both hardware and software, in the form of PCs, servers, networks, telecommunications, programs, and familiar operating systems such as Windows and Unix. It is the way this technology has been applied that gives the Internet its unique place in the history of computing and in the future.

What has ultimately established the Internet as such a major force is its availability and accessibility to anyone with a computer, modem and phone line. It is now commonplace to have an e-mail address and Web site in much the same way as a phone and fax number. This is causing sociological changes, too.

The rapid pace of change in these areas is making it increasingly important that IT professionals keep abreast of these technologies; not only for themselves, but also for the businesses, organisations and individuals they will be servicing. It is this highly dynamic market that makes it more difficult to be successful in the IT

Howard Gerlis

Howard Gerlis, MBCS, MIMIS is Chairman of the BCS Internet Specialist Group and was until recently Chairman of the BCS North London Branch. He is also a member of the BCS Technical Board and sits on the Membership Assessment Panel. His entire career, since graduating from the University of Westminster in 1976, has been in the field of commercial computing and he has a background of projects in computers and Information Systems (IT) at both the strategic and technical levels. In 1993 Howard set up Andor Information Technology Ltd, a team specialising in software development, networks, communications, Internet, technical support, training, documentation and consultancy. He has written articles for several publications.

arena because choosing the right set of skills and qualifications is not a precise science when there is a constantly changing focus.

However, understanding the scope of the technology now, and looking at how it has emerged in the past, can give us some indication as to how it might progress in the future. There are definitely certain basic skills that not only traverse the different technologies themselves, but also withstand the changes over time.

The skills required for these areas are mainly require those of a technical nature; candidates should not, therefore, be afraid of becoming involved in the detail of computer systems.

The buzzword of the moment is 'e-commerce', enabling us to use the Internet for buying, selling, and general communication, online, instead of using traditional methods. However, it must be realised that it is still normal commerce; the main difference is simply the medium by which the commerce is transacted. A jazzy Web page isn't enough – it must function well enough to allow the customer to find information and place an order easily.

Skills

Every major change brings both opportunity and threat. Every major communication revolution not only makes the process of business faster and cheaper but also brings with it new avenues. The World Wide Web removes traditional national barriers to global commerce and enables even the smallest enterprise to have a 'shop window' open to the world.

"The World Wide Web removes traditional national barriers to global commerce..."

The Internet encompasses several different areas of computer technology and therefore presents a broad range of opportunities for the aspiring individual wanting to move into those areas:
- Software system design and development
- Server, and other hardware, support
- Networks
- Operating systems
- Telecommunications
- Security

More specifically, in addition to Internet installation and support, the World Wide Web provides opportunities in:
- Web design and development
- Software development
- Training
- Graphic design and animation
- Video capture
- Electronic commerce
- Publishing
- Law

At the more technical level, there is great demand for many proprietary skills in specific product-based areas. It may well be worth considering aiming to build up expertise in one or more of these products. It's important, though, to be aware that there is the danger that what may be in vogue one month may be out of date the next.

Web page development and design

To actually design a Web site requires, ideally, a mix of design and technology skills, though you would not necessarily be expected to have both, as it is more likely that you would be working as part of a team. In the early days of Web construction, HTML (Hypertext Markup Language), the tagging language of Web pages, had to be coded by hand. Nowadays, sophisticated graphical editors are available to make that task much easier. They generate the HTML code automatically. In addition, Web pages will have many purely graphical elements such as pictures, photos and illustrations, animations and for these, a good knowledge of the major graphic software design tools is useful, plus a natural flair for design.
- HTML
- Web editors eg Dreamweaver, Frontpage, GoLive
- Graphic Design tools, Quark, Adobe Photoshop, Illustrator, Freehand
- Special design tools: Shockwave, Flash

Programming

A normal Web page is generally a static piece of information; software programming tools will typically allow Web sites to be more dynamic, allowing for online forms, user interactivity and enabling database, or other, connectivity between the server and the user.

- Java
- JavaScript
- CGI Scripting, Vbscript, Perl

Database connectivity

Linking Web pages to server-end databases is now becoming an important aspect of interactivity. It allows for instant up-to-date information to be displayed; users can update the databases directly, and most important, actual Web pages are themselves generated from the information held on the database, obviating the need for every page to be manually customised or maintained; only the database has to be updated. Active Server Pages (ASP) is currently the commonly used approach for this area.

- Oracle, Cold Fusion, Access, SQL, ASP
- Active Server Pages (ASP)

New technologies

The mobile phone is fast opening up a whole new vista of Internet-enabled technology with Web-based information being delivered via the wireless application protocol (WAP), using a special variant of HTML, known as WML. This allows the text portions of Web pages to be presented on cellular phones and personal digital assistants (PDAs) via wireless access.

XML, Extensible Markup Language, is a flexible way to create common information formats and share both the format and the data on the World Wide Web, and elsewhere. XML can be used by any individual or group of individuals or companies that want to share information in a consistent way.

- XML
- WAP

Personal attributes

How an individual relates to this area of IT is as important as the actual skills themselves. Therefore you should have the right character to be effective and enjoy working with Internet technologies. These would include:

- technical bias;
- ability to deal with system problems;
- good oral and written skills;
- tenacity and resilience;
- understanding of design and logic.

Career development

It can be said that once skills have been gained in a particular area of computing, it is easier to translate that knowledge into another area. This is generally true of most aspects of the IT profession, but the sheer pace of change also makes those skills become quickly out of date. Continuous learning is imperative and joining a scheme such as the BCS Continuing Professional Development Scheme is one way of addressing this; it ensures you are kept abreast of the latest developments in IT and have records to prove it.

The overall opportunities for working within the Internet field are tremendous and continually growing. It is vital to have a basic grounding in IT plus a broad academic and some practical knowledge of implementing such systems. This can be followed by specialisation in a particular area by further study or on-the-job experience.

The future?

Who would have believed only a few years ago that the Internet phenomenon would happen? We can learn from these recent experiences is that it is certain the technology will become better and cheaper. It will be a combination of elements that will affect the type of changes we will see, in everything from government legislation to faster telephone lines. However, it is always important to remember that many of the new products we see in computing technology are due as much to commercial competition as to technological advances.

It is clear that the Internet will become more consumer-oriented with services being delivered into the home. Already we are seeing video-on-demand, Internet via the TV, digital broadcasting, Web on mobile phones and use of the Internet for voice calls.

The opportunities for the aspiring IT professional are limited only by the imagination.

Networks and communications

Communications is the field of information technology that deals with the exchange of information between computers or people. Communications had, of course, a history of almost a century before programmable computers existed, based on analogue or very rudimentary digital techniques, and restricted to telephony and teletype communications.

Changes and advances in computer technology have made possible great progress in the fields of data communication over networks accessed through and controlled by computers. High-speed digital signal processing has made multimedia communications practical and affordable. Communications also travel by radio via satelites.

It is no longer sufficient for an organisation, big or small, simply to have stand-alone computers: the expectation is that several computers are connected together to share information, optimise the use of peripheral equipment and connect to the world at large. Networks range from very large-scale public networks to very small-scale private networks or even single PCs with a phone line and modem or connected to each other via a cable. Installations of cable television networks, telephone company networks and high-speed cellular networks can be exploited. This encompasses two main technologies that today are closely related, those of networking and the Internet. (The Internet and its career opportunities are covered elsewhere in the Guide.)

Howard Gerlis

Howard Gerlis, MBCS, MIMIS is Chairman of the BCS Internet Specialist Group and was until recently Chairman of the BCS North London Branch. He is also a member of the BCS Technical Board and sits on the Membership Assessment Panel. His entire career, since graduating from the University of Westminster in 1976, has been in the field of commercial computing and he has a background of projects in computers and Information Systems (IS) at both the strategic and technical levels. In 1993 Howard set up Andor Information Technology Ltd, a team specialising in software development, networks, communications, Internet, technical support, training, documentation and consultancy. He has written articles for several publications.

The skills required for communications and networks are mainly those of a technical nature, and candidates should not be afraid of becoming involved in the detail of computer systems. The rapid pace of change in these areas is making it increasingly important that IT professionals keep abreast of new technologies, not only for themselves but also for the businesses, organisations and individuals they will be servicing. However, choosing the right set of skills and qualifications is not a precise science when there is a constantly changing focus. Nevertheless, there are definitely certain basic skills that not only traverse the different technologies themselves, but also withstand the changes over time.

Networking

Before the advent of the PC, nearly all mainframe and minicomputers had a fundamental networking approach, usually in the form of a central machine with many users connected to it, there being little or no processing at the users' end. All data was held, and processing carried out, centrally.

With the emergence of the PC, local, unconnected processing became possible. However, this presented the problems of sharing both information and facilities such as printers, so there has been a significant growth in computer networks and data communications plus the resultant growth in the telecommunications infrastructure to support this. To accommodate the exponential growth in traffic demand, backbone networks had to be rebuilt; they use optical fibre links, new transfer and switching methods and new methods of addressing the hundreds of millions of devices and of routing information between them in a resilient and flexible way.

Local area networks

The technology of networking applies not only to the Internet, but also to connectivity within an organisation. In this scenario there is no standard approach and several proprietary networking systems straddle the market. This contrasts with the Internet which is based on a common protocol to allow connection between different systems.

Typically such networks are known as Local Area Networks (LAN), and are usually based on hard-wired cabling, as opposed to the telephone system used for the Internet. The simplest network can link a small number of computers with no particular computer controlling the data across the systems.

As the need for more users, more shared devices, larger amounts of data

and better security becomes necessary, a server-based network is the best solution. The system is controlled by a central machine, the 'server', but most processing can still be carried out at the user's workstation computer. The resources of the network, such as for printing or obtaining data, are used only when necessary. Known also as client–server, the network and applications intelligently divide the processing between the server and the user, or 'client', to optimise the usage of the entire network.

Other, less obvious, environments where connection is required are point of sale tills in retail outlets, and sensor devices connected to a central control mechanism, such as controlling industrial equipment and bank cash machines. These may require somewhat specialised systems, not commonly found elsewhere. Novell Netware, Microsoft Windows NT and Unix are all major network systems of this type.

These local systems can connect to other networks, forming a Wide Area Network (WAN), to telecommunication services, such as fax, or to the Internet.

There is great demand for many proprietary skills in specific product-based areas, and it may well be worth considering aiming to build up expertise in one or more of these products. It's important, though, to be aware that there is the danger that what may be in vogue one month may be out of date the next. It is difficult for the individual to decide how to aim for the best skills and knowledge to target this fragmented technology.

Career development

The various different types of software, hardware, protocols and standards used to allow computers to communicate all bring with them the need for different skills. It can be said that once skills have been gained in a particular area of computing or specific data communications, it is easier to translate that knowledge into another area. This is generally true of most aspects of the IT profession, but the sheer pace of change also makes those skills quickly out of date. Continuous learning is imperative. Joining a Continuing Professional Development Scheme such as that operated by the BCS is one way of addressing this; it ensures you are kept abreast of the latest developments in IT and have records to prove it.

It is easy to find an area which suits a particular interest and these may consist of:

- network system planning and design;
- telephony and telecommunications;
- hardware installation, linking networks;
- network software development and support;
- security;
- cabling;
- connectivity to other devices and services;
- network management and optimisation;
- backup systems.

> "The overall opportunities in communication and networks are tremendous and continually growing."

The overall opportunities in communication and networks are tremendous and continually growing. It is vital to have a basic grounding in IT plus a broad academic and practical knowledge of implementing such systems, then specialise in a particular area by further study or on-the-job experience.

Personal attributes

Apart from interpersonal communication skills, listening and imparting information, you will need to have competent system design and technical skills and be adept at dealing with system problems. Tenacity and resilience are, therefore, two personal characteristics you should possess.

The future?

It seems that the technology will continue to become better and cheaper. Economic growth is a key factor and the pressures for many of the new developments in computing technology come from the needs of commercial competition.

The future of mobile technology

The speed at which mobile technology changes can be difficult to keep up with; mobile device companies are constantly introducing new handsets, new services and new standards. Just what devices and technologies will be available in the coming months and how will they help to improve communications for people on the move? Furthermore, what are the implications for those who are looking at a profession in IT, especially in an area such as mobile communications, which seems to be changing every day?

We are accustomed to the mobile phone, that enables voice communication between two mobile parties together with voicemail thrown in. The newest mobile devices will do much more than that. We hear about second generation WAP phones on sale, two and a half generation technologies such as GPRS are expected and third generation UMTS will be with us in 2002. What do these terms mean?

Anne-Marie Molloy

Anne-Marie Molloy is a Senior Manager in Vodafone's Products and Services department. She manages major projects and programmes, sometimes cross-divisional but always with an IT bias. She is currently working on a project that looks at Vodafone's Independent Distribution Strategy. Anne-Marie was recently appointed as the Account Manager for Vodafone's Commercial and Marketing division which means she is responsible for making sure that the IT department's relationship with them is successful. If that wasn't enough, Anne-Marie is a line manager, looking after a small team of project managers. Her qualifications include IMS (Dip) and DMS. Anne-Marie is 35 years old, is married and has four children.

to receive the information most suited to customers needs and interests.

Wireless application protocol

WAP phones provide a direct connection to Internet services via the mobile handset. The set which incorporates a larger than average screen, navigation buttons and an in-built microbrowser, eliminating the need for a PC or laptop. Connection to the Internet is made through a mobile Internet portal service provider.

WAP offers customers a massive range of information services – from global news, sports results and finance to travel schedule information and weather reports. These services can be personalised in order

Universal mobile telecommunications service – UMTS

The evolution from second-generation GSM networks through to UMTS or third generation (3G) heralds the greatest revolution in mobile communications. With predicted data rates of up to 2 Mbs, 3G mobile phones will be able to receive Internet data, video communications and graphics faster than on a traditional fixed line, even receive television broadcasts.

The introduction of this technology is not set to happen immediately; complete services will not come online until around

2002. In the interim, so-called 2.5G services such as General Packet Radio Services (GPRS) will be available.

General packet radio services

Bringing customers high-speed data services and enhanced internet capabilities over existing GSM mobile networks, GPRS is a data transmission technology operating at rates significantly faster than the current GSM rate and approaching the fastest fixed dial-up speeds of ISDN. The technology offers more reliable access and a permanent connection to the Internet that means consumers will only incur a charge when data is sent or received.

Users of mobile phones are therefore eagerly awaiting 2002 when the introduction of 3G mobile phones with full multimedia capabilities will offer true wireless Internet capability for the first time.

The mobile workplace

So the technology is changing – and rapidly. In my opnion, there will be three main areas within the IT sector that will be different for graduates in the telecom industry.

Job hopping!

Graduates will be less and less likely to stay in one team or on one technology for more than a couple of years. In order to survive, graduates will need to be prepared to renew their technical knowledge every five years or less! Indeed, in the early part of graduates' careers, you can expect to move teams/technologies every six months.

Change of philosophy

Buy not build will be an important philosophy. IT professionals will need a skill set based around selecting and working with other organisations – that is, how to get the best from them and how to integrate their services.

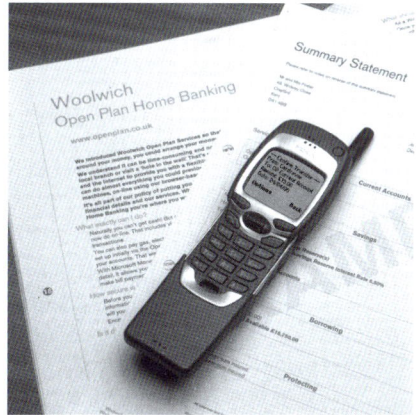

Knowing the market

Two and a half and 3G technology will broaden the mobile world to embrace other devices and activities, for example Bluetooth or personal organisers. Success will come from being able to understand consumer trends and behaviours and apply the technology to best effect. Mostly these will be large-scale, mainstream offerings; there won't be much room for playing with the technology for its own sake!

> "Success will come from being able to understand consumer trends and behaviours and apply the technology to best effect."

Mobile technology itself is evolving so fast that there simply won't be the need for armies of programmers; for example, many management information tools will be operable by the user. As a result the old career path of programmer to systems analyst to project leader won't be there. Instead there will probably be more opportunities for facilitation/coordination/system integration roles, maybe leading to cross-functional project management. There will also be more emphasis on people understanding the business/commercial environment they work in as well as being technically competent.

Investment banking

What is investment banking?

Investment banking is an umbrella term used to refer to a range of business activities connected with financial markets. Activities include assisting companies to issue shares or bonds, trading and clearing these securities in the financial markets and managing investment funds. Underpinning these activities is the research into companies, markets and national economies that drives investment decisions, so every investment bank has its own research teams.

How do investment banks use technology?

Most aspects of computer science are used somewhere in the modern investment bank: Web-based customer interfaces, fault-tolerant real-time trading systems, database processing, complex mathematical modelling, even knowledge-based and adaptive systems. As well as business analysts, designers and developers, the huge computing infrastructures need systems, network and database administrators too.

Financial institutions have been quick to adapt to the Internet revolution. Online banking and Internet share-dealing have become routine. Today the cycle of change is around business-to-business e-commerce, with fund managers, brokers and stock exchanges linking up electronically to create global 24-hour markets that will allow investment capital to flow seamlessly around the world.

David Morgan

David Morgan is a Vice President at Merrill Lynch, working as a manager in the Equity Finance Technology group. He has worked in the City for a total of 8 years and has a degree in Philosophy and Literature from Warwick University.

Yet the core elements of investment bank technology are still the trading and settlement systems. These need constant enhancement to stay current because of the rapid rate of change in world financial markets. Share trading is booming and investors are looking to invest worldwide, not just at home. These factors are driving a wave of change and consolidation which is keeping IT departments busier than ever.

Also in recent years there has been tremendous growth in what are called derivative products, such as futures and options. These are the often complex investments which are based in some way on another investment. Understanding these products and modelling the risk and return from them is a highly technical and mathematical challenge.

What is the future of technology in financial services?

The flow of news and market data is the lifeblood of a trading floor. Once trades have been dealt they are reported, confirmed and agreed with the other party, then securities and cash are settled, accounts are updated and the securities are kept in safe custody; yet today all of this is done electronically, by data flowing through systems. The investment bank has become an information processing organisation.

It is conceivable that in the next 10 years all exchange trading floors may be replaced by electronic markets, that many trading decisions may be made by black-box computer systems, that the Internet may make financial advisers obsolete and that all national stock markets may dissolve; but it is inconceivable that the global financial organisations will stop using computer systems and networks, or stop looking for competitive advantage from the strength of their technology solutions.

What's working in IT in the City like?

Investment banks employ a wide range of IT specialists, so if you are bright and hard-working then there could be a role for you. There is a lot of diversity in the staff, with people from many backgrounds. All the main investment banks in the UK are located in the City of London, however, so you are unlikely to find a job in one unless you are prepared to work there. Since all the major firms are global, once you have experience there may be opportunities to move to other financial centres worldwide.

It is a fast-changing and highly successful service industry. The philosophy is to invest money and grow, not to downsize and cost-cut. This combination of a dynamic business environment and significant investment makes it a superb place for an IT career.

The rewards, including the financial packages, are excellent, particularly once you have a few years' finance sector experience, but it can be a pressurised and demanding environment. A high level of

commitment and a strong focus on results is the norm. This is not the right sector if you are looking for a quiet life or to do pure research.

What are the IT job opportunities?

Since there is a lot of reliance on networks and distributed computing, it is an ideal field for network planners and systems architects. These roles need skilled technical people with practical experience, so one way in is to start as a systems engineer on the support side, helping to install, configure and support the network and application infrastructure.

Skilled business system developers are also needed. Knowledge of the financial sector is not always necessary but is a great asset, which creates a chicken-and-egg problem for new graduates. One solution is to take a financial markets course if offered as part of your degree, or a post-graduate diploma from a business school.

How do I get started?

Many investment banks are not household names, so investigate who the main players are. The City pages of quality daily newspapers are one place to start.

Consider applying to the graduate training programmes which are offered by all big investment banks. These will give you a flying start with business-specific training and carefully selected job roles. You will need a good degree, not necessarily in computing although you will be expected to be numerate. Remember that for these programmes employers are thinking about your future leadership potential, not just your technical skills. Qualities that are often sought are drive, an ability to see things through, team-working skills, adaptability and good communication. Think about how you have demonstrated these attributes during your university or work career before the interview!

If you apply for a graduate training post and really like what you see of the company but don't get selected for the graduate programme, then consider writing back to enquire about the possibility of being hired directly for a vacancy. Remember that determination counts for a lot to recruiters and that for your career the important thing is to get some experience.

Financial services

Twenty-first century financial services

IT is particularly important in the financial services industry, where the financial futures of individuals and organisations alike are administered. Customers can be won and lost on the ability of a financial services organisation to provide an efficient and accurate service to its customers. Effective information systems handling large volumes of data play a crucial role in making this happen.

As the world enters a new millennium, the future of information technology in financial services organisations is guaranteed. Many, including familiar household names such as banks, building societies and insurance companies, have only begun to scratch the surface of the possibilities that new technologies can bring to their organisations. The companies who understand these possibilities and who exploit the emerging technologies appropriately are the ones who will retain and attract customers.

Twenty-first century customer services

We, as consumers, are becoming more demanding. Many of us expect to be able to access our bank accounts instantly, at our own convenience, without the need to speak to a customer services person. Others, who prefer personal contact, still expect to be able to have telephone contact with their product provider without the need to visit a branch. The more traditional customers who visit their branch

Nick McMenemy

Nick McMenemy BA (Hons) is IS Graduate Recruitment Manager at Standard Life. He joined their Information Systems Division in 1997. As part of their trainee programme he spent a year as a systems programmer working within an IBM operating system environment. He subsequently spent a year as a systems developer writing applications for Standard Life's Marketing Division before taking up his current role.

would like to be able to check their balance, make deposits and withdraw funds literally at the touch of a button, even if it is the branch staff pressing it. The staff, also users of the technology, also expect information about the customer and about products to be available at their fingertips.

Customers may be private or corporate and both are looking for speed of transaction. Large numbers of customers are no longer prepared to visit their branch in order to request transfers of funds between accounts or buy financial products, for example the purchase of traditionally more complex products such as mortgages and loans. These transactions can be completed in minutes over the phone without the customer ever visiting the mortgage provider in person.

E-commerce, based on telephony and Internet technologies, has enabled financial services companies as well as other businesses to offer and transact business electronically. E-commerce allows cus-

tomers to have, in many cases, access to their accounts and insurance policies 24 hours a day, 7 days a week. They can purchase new products and open accounts at their own convenience, in their offices or in the comfort of their own homes with confidence in the security of the system.

With the advent of the Internet and the World Wide Web, financial organisations now operate in a truly global marketplace. Trading no longer starts at 9am and finishes at 5 – customers may live in different countries or even continents, and expect their product providers to reflect this.

IT, communications and information systems have made all this possible.

Twenty-first century technologies

Large financial services companies have traditionally been very heavily dependent upon mainframe technology to store and process data and support business processes. Mainframes allow very large quantities of data to be processed rapidly and are extremely secure and robust – for many large organisations, each with many thousands of customers, the mainframe remains the 'backbone' of their IT systems.

However, most companies have for some years been developing client–server and desktop technology solutions to complement the mainframe and provide a more helpful interface for customer services staff. The mainframe remains the main repository of data, while friendly user interfaces transform this data into easily readable and meaningful information.

Internet technologies allow customers to access this information directly, in a clearly understandable format, enabling them to check their bank balance, apply for a credit card, arrange home insurance etc. Advances in telephony systems combined with Internet and WAP technologies will further increase the number of ways in which financial services companies can communicate and transact business with their customers.

Twenty-first century opportunities

Financial services continue to account for an increasingly large share of the economies of the UK, Europe and the USA. Competitive advantage in this extremely fast-moving sector can be gained through the implementation of effective IT solutions which improve business efficiency and customer service and reduce operating costs.

Implementing these technologies requires talented and skilled IT staff with a good understanding of the potential benefits IT can bring to an organisation. The market for IT staff remains very competitive with many organisations seeking to grow their IT or IS department to reflect its importance to the rest of the business. This is an excellent sector to join as a trainee, with most organisations providing extensive technical training and personal development opportunities to bring new graduates quickly up to speed. The learning continues after the initial induction period to reflect the ever-changing technologies, and any individual or organisation who fails to recognise the importance of continuous training and development will be left behind.

As new products are launched and existing ones enhanced, so the systems that support them must be created and amended. Systems analysts work closely with customer service and marketing teams to design new systems. Analysts write the specifications for how these systems should be created and development staff write the programs to support these designs.

IT hardware and software must also exist before these programs can be run. It is the role of operations staff to build and install mainframe, server, desktop, Internet and telephony technologies and the supporting network software that links them to each other.

Financial services remains a very fast-moving, dynamic and competitive industry in which to work, especially in an IT or IT-related role. There are lots of opportunities to work with many different technologies and develop an outstanding career, picking up valuable skills and experiences along the way.

Most financial services organisations give information about recruitment and training schemes on their Web sites, so start your research by exploring the Web.

Frequently asked questions

Q Are the Microsoft qualifications (MCSE) the best way to get in?

A They provide one way to enter IT. However, employers will be reluctant to recruit you unless you can prove that you are competent. It is not enough that you attended a course and passed at the end of it. Make sure that you provide evidence that you have completed some design exercises for someone other than your trainers or your own use.

Q I am seeking a career change OR I have just been made redundant, and am interested in a career in IT. How do I start?

A Find some means of demonstrating that you have competence in an aspect of IT. Look at advertisements for local jobs in IT and see what skills they are seeking. Look at small and medium-sized organisations as well as large ones. Look for courses offered at your local college, rather than spending a lot on commercial courses with no promise of employment at the end. Once you are employed, even at a low level of seniority, it will be easier to move up the ladder.

Q I need assistance in funding/sponsorship for my IT course. Where can I go for help?

A *The Computer User's Yearbook*, and other Guides you will find in your local library, in the Reference section, will give names of companies which may help.

Sometimes your college or university department can help, as they will have contacts in business, industry and commerce. Another source is the Internet: many companies have sections specifically aimed at students, and equally many have feedback facilities for you to ask questions directly.

Q Are the NVQ qualifications high enough to gain employment in IT?

A Employment in IT is at several levels of seniority. An NVQ in IT demonstrates that you have a level of competency in IT and this is recognised by employers.

Q I am interested in starting a work placement which will lead to a job. Where can I go about finding this?

A If you are doing this from school as part of work-based learning, speak to your careers department. Alternatively, try your local careers office, or the job centre. Try writing to the personnel department of large employers, as they may offer work experience opportunities and sponsorships for degrees and diplomas. Also look at WorkLink on the BCS Web site which is specifically designed to help students find industrial placements.

Q Can you provide a list of IT job opportunities in my area, or where can I go for this?

A For school-leavers, consult your school careers department, and the local careers office.

For those with seniority, develop your personal networking contacts and attend local BCS Branch meetings.

Consult the local press as well as *Computing* and *Computer Weekly*, whose job ads cover the whole country. Look at small and medium-sized organisations as well as large ones. Again, don't forget the Internet!

Q Do you feel that there is a shortage of IT trained staff? Is this the best field for me to train in?

A Government-funded surveys have confirmed that there is a serious shortage of skilled IT staff. However, see the comments under Question 1.

Q I have just graduated and am looking for advice on seeking employment in IT. What advice can you give?

A Many employers recruit graduates with degrees other than in computing, and provide the IT training as career development. Look at local advertisements, and use the Internet to locate suitable companies.

Attend the Engineering Recruitment Shows sponsored by the Institution of Electrical Engineers/Institution of Mechanical Engineers and the IT recruitment show sponsored by the BCS/IEE.

If there are no local firms recruiting at present, consider a postgraduate course in IT, or a training course, but see the comments under Question 1.

Q What specific qualifications are necessary to enter the IT profession?

A In fact, no specific qualifications are necessary, but to qualify for professional status in IT three elements are needed: education, training and responsible experience. The education could be provided by a degree in, say, computing or software engineering, preferably accredited by the BCS. Responsible experience will come through a scheme such as Continuing Professional Development, run by the BCS.

Employers will also recruit graduates from other disciplines and provide the IT training later. To enter at a lower level of seniority (and lower salary), there are HNCs and HNDs in the computing area.

Q I am interested in a career in technical support. What advice can you give?

A There are HNC and HND courses in computing. The HNC is a part-time course, while the HND is full-time but may include work experience which provides evidence of your skills. These qualifications will go some way towards making a start in computer hardware or software support. Network support is a specialised role, to which you can aspire once you have become proficient in the first two areas.

Hardware support staff are often recruited from a technical electronic background with an HNC or HND qualification, or a sandwich degree course, as employers tend to ask for experience.

Q Are Computeach certificates a way to get into a career in IT?

A Computeach students taking a Computeach course in preparation for the BCS Professional Examination would be eligible to become student members of BCS. Otherwise they are seen as IT users' qualifications.

Did you know?

IT services account for more than 10% of all new jobs created in the UK in the past 3 years and the number is still growing (*Skills 99: IT Skills Summary report to the DTI* by Matthew Dixon).

The employed IT workforce is split between suppliers of IT and user companies, 30% in suppliers and the rest in users.

Eighty per cent of the IT workforce has at least GCSEs or equivalent, and over one-third have first or higher degrees.

The skills most used by graduates in employment were oral communication, interpersonal skills, ability to prioritise tasks, and time management.

Graduates who are satisfied with their careers are most often those with degrees in engineering and technology, business studies, maths and computing (according to *Working Out: Short report for the HE Careers Services Unit* by the Institute for Employment Research, Warwick University).

By the end of 1995, after 10 years of service, mobile phones accounted for 3.8% of all telecoms traffic. This rose to over 12.5% of all traffic by the end of 1999. It has been projected that mobiles will account for 25% of all telecoms minutes used by 2007.

Business conducted online is increasing – by the end of 2000 worldwide e-commerce is predicted to grow to $1 billion.

Over 70% of UK businesses of all sizes have access to the Internet. Over 40% of people in the UK have direct access to the Internet at work from their own PCs (up from 30% in 1998 according to IDC's Global IT Survey 1999).

Ninety-eight per cent accuracy is claimed for the latest speech recognition software. It has taken the IT community 30 years to achieve these levels.

Current supercomputers can perform a million million operations per second.

From atoms to bits

Only 40 years ago the dominant tools of the IT practitioner were the slide rule, screwdriver and soldering iron. Being a computer engineer meant knowing about hardware, software, programming and a host of input/output devices, including arrays of toggle switches, teletypes, tape and card readers. When I entered the profession just 30 years ago computers still used discrete transistors and tubes, and the VDU was just arriving on the scene. Machines the size of a house were distinctly user unfriendly, and far less powerful than my personal digital assistant (PDA) today. At that time it was still possible for an individual to know a great deal about every aspect of the entire system right down to a component level. Today, everything is infinitely more powerful and complex, and of necessity we have all become so specialised.

It is no longer possible for any one human to understand every aspect of the hardware, software and system of a pocket calculator, let alone a laptop or networks of computing machines. Individuals now focus down to particular chip fabrication techniques, packaging methods, interconnects, thermal management, operating systems, languages, application sets or interface devices. So I think we can now safely assume that no one understands IT. But does it matter in a world where the next 30 years will see machines creating even better machines to push us further out of the loop? I think not!

Peter Cochrane

Peter Cochrane is Chief Technologist BT and holds the Collier Chair for the Public Understanding of Science & Technology, University of Bristol.

What wonderful opportunities now face people entering the IT profession. In 1979 when I completed my PhD the 3 years of study had involved a lot of mathematics, small amounts of computational effort and huge amounts of experimentation. Today that study could be completed in 3 months using my laptop. This machine is far more powerful than all the computing power used by NASA to put a man on the moon. My R&D team and PhD students now complete more work in a week than was possible in a year just a few decades ago. Moreover, hardly a week goes by without some profound discovery emerging in every aspect of IT. Already we have the first inklings that artificial life may change the nature of computing forever. I don't suppose for one moment we will be breeding new forms of wordprocessor, but I am fairly certain that from breeding new forms of algorithm today, we will rapidly move on to create powerful new agents for data organisation, logistics, searching, modelling, design and management. As our hardware and software becomes increasingly networked and biological in its realisation and operation, we will require new skills to understand the implications.

"Already we have the first inklings that artificial life may change the nature of computing forever."

In recent months we have seen ships of the US Navy, using an experimental operating system extended beyond 50 million lines of code, rendered dead in the water by their software. By accidentally typing in a zero denominator, a rating on the bridge of one ship not only disabled the host, but also related ships on the network. We come from a direction of creating steep hierarchies of huge complexity to do very simple things. Mother Nature on the other hand employs almost no hierarchy, and incredibly simple software, to do unbelievably complex things. A society of ants only requires 400 lines of code in each entity, having only 200 neurons. We would be hard pressed to create such a society using our computers and traditional software. And yet, by simply aping nature we have not only reproduced ant colonies, but network systems of previously unbelievable robustness that replace 1.6M lines of code with less than 1,000.

> "Our world is making a transition from being dominated by atoms to being dominated by Bits, from being randomly ordered to being mathematically chaotic."

My laptop computer is computationally far more powerful than any ant, but a lot dumber. Why doesn't it exhibit true intelligence? Well, it suffers from gross sensory deprivation and an inability to reconfigure its logic. In biological systems of great intelligence, the sensory system, neural connectivity and configuration are key elements in the intelligence equation. In this respect there are 4 vital words we use every day without any notion of their meaning, quantification or definition: life, intelligence, complexity and scalability. It is vital for our future that we fully understand these concepts if we are to realise high-performance and robust systems.

Our world is making a transition from being dominated by atoms to being dominated by Bits, from being randomly ordered to being mathematically chaotic. Chaos is now brought about by coffee, ladders and train cancellations. At an international conference coffee arrives at 1015, and as 4,000 people stream out of the hall, 250 mobile phones come out in less than 30 seconds. Then the system collapses. On a major motorway a ladder falls off the back of a truck into the fast lane and every car that swerves to miss that ladder hits 999 and brings down the emergency service for over 3 hours. Train and plane cancellations have a similar effect. Everywhere in our society, people expect instant gratification and want the same things at the same time. It is no accident that we have yo-yo famines, and every parent trying to buy Cabbage Patch Dolls or Buzz Lightyear within the same few weeks at Christmas. Mass communication and connectivity mean everyone can see and decide on the same things in the same epoch. The challenge for young people now entering the profession is to understand this paradigm and find the means to engineer robust solutions. Technology now advances at a visibly exponential rate and we now live in a world with more machines online than people. In 2010 we will see 95% of the world's bit traffic originated and terminated by machines and just 5% by people talking.

As a society and a species our dependence on technology is now complete. Switch off the networks and/or the computers and there would be no heat, light, power, transport, clothing or food. No nothing! We can no longer support the population of the planet without complex technology. Everything from farming to the production of computers themselves involves a linked and totally dependent chain of communication networks and computers. Our technology is like a ratchet – it goes one way in the direction of increased dependence, and so does the responsibility of every professional in the chain. It is critical therefore that we get it right; we cannot afford serious mistakes. The opportunity for triggering some minor or major catastrophe is always with us, and so IT calls for the highest levels of dedication and professionalism.

> "The opportunity for triggering some minor or major catastrophe is always with us, and so IT calls for the highest levels of dedication and professionalism."

So, what could I advise those who are now considering IT as a career for the next 30 years? Well, unlike previous generations who focused on one particular discipline, I would suggest a broader approach. Instead of just studying IT, newcomers should also contemplate the inclusion of biological systems, life and intelligent forms, human interaction, psychology, and at least a dash of mathematics and economics. Unlike any other time in our history, we need people to be more holistic, capable and adaptable. Certainly we should still be looking to create specialists at all levels and in all the arenas of IT; in fact, we need people who are almost 'delta functions' in their knowledge, very deep and very narrow. But they also need a broader appreciation of how they and their expertise fit into the bigger picture. As technology accelerates, the narrowness of specialisation will deepen, change, and change rapidly. Also, systems and applications will come and go faster and IT professionals will have to be fleeter of mind and foot.

The past 30 years of my life in IT have been incredibly rich in experience, discovery, realisation and excitement; I would not have missed it for anything. But I am sure that those of you now entering the profession will experience even more – just gain from the past and contribute positively to the future – and most of all, enjoy!

Contractors

Current numbers and options

Hard figures are difficult to come by, but current estimates of the number of freelance staff in IT are of the order of 50,000, which is possibly around 20% of those in the profession. Current employment trends indicate that this percentage could rise even higher during the course of the next decade, so there is a strong possibility that many of you reading this Guide will follow this route at some stage in your career. The old concept of a 'job for life' disappeared a long time ago; even if you do not move into contracting, you are likely to have a number of employers during the course of your working life.

The opportunity to 'go contract' will not usually be viable until after 2 or 3 years in 'permanent' employment, as contractors are hired for their existing skills profile – they are not trained by the client to perform a specific job role. This does place the onus on the contractor to keep their skills profile marketable, as there is no employer (other than their own 'one-person' company) to plan out their career route. Schemes such as the British Computer Society's new Continuing Professional Development scheme will go a long way towards meeting this need.

Many of you will become contractors through choice, others possibly because of redundancy in later life. Unfortunately, an election pledge to make ageism illegal has been watered down to a voluntary code, without the force of law behind it. Although this may seem a long way away in the future for you when you read this,

Mike Cullen
Mike Cullen has been a contractor for the past 17 years and Chairman of the Independent Computer Contractors Specialist Group of the BCS since its inaugural AGM in April 1990. He is an elected member of the BCS Council and active on several BCS Boards on behalf of contractors.

some firms are reluctant to hire 'permanent' staff in IT over the age of 35, and many older workers have moved into contracting as a result of this view.

How to find work

Most contractors find work through an agency (of whom there are in excess of 200). There are several publications filled with adverts aimed specifically at contractors, and these days any agency worth its salt has its own Web site. There are also several large job sites, where several dozen agencies post job vacancies. This mechanism works well, as IT departments do not want to be bombarded with hundreds of individual CVs, but prefer to issue their requirements to several preferred suppliers, and let them perform the search for suitable contractors. Agencies belonging to the Computer Division of REC (the Recruitment and Employment Confederation) adhere to a Code of Practice, which safeguards the contractor's interests, and you would be well advised to check that any agency you use is a member before registering with them.

Once a contract is secured, the contract takes the form of two 'back to back' agreements, one between the contractor's own company and the agency, and one between the client and the agency. The role, which you perform at the client site, will almost always be determined by your previous career history, as that is usually the basis upon which you are taken on. Once a site knows you, you might be able to move into a fresh field if the client doesn't have the expertise in-house. They might well feel that with your knowledge of the company, it is preferable to use you, rather than to bring in a new contractor who is familiar with the technology, but not with the company. In contracting, there is an element of making your own luck. The planned Professional Experience Record scheme from the BCS will be a major benefit in enabling this sort of career redirection to be formally documented.

The rewards

Rates for contractors vary according to their skills. For example, PC support can currently carry over £500 per week while those with seniority and rare, new skills such as e-commerce expertise can earn up to £5,000 per week. These compare with average annual salaries in permanent posts of around £20,000 for PC support and £45,000 for systems analysts. Experience is an important factor and first-time contractors can expect to be offered about 10 to 15% less.

If this sounds enticing, you do need to be aware that you are responsible for providing all the benefits that you normally receive from an employer. Pension plans, permanent health insurance, life insurance, critical illness cover and possibly private health insurance all need to be arranged. You will not get holiday pay! You would also be advised to make provision for possible periods of 'resting'; economic cycles can occasionally lead to an extended break between contracts. The only statutory requirement is for your company to have employer's liability insurance – this is normally provided with public liability insurance, and is quite inexpensive. It pays to seek out professional financial advice – don't sign up with the first salesman who gets hold of your telephone number.

Recent government legislation (IR35) will make contracting less financially attractive for the majority of contractors. More information can be found at www.ir35update.co.uk. A legal challenge to the new rules has been mounted, so it is advisable to check the current situation if you are thinking of taking up contracting.

How it works

In the UK, most contractors work through the auspices of their own limited liability company (technically they are the managing director!). The Inland Revenue prefer this to self-employed status, as salary is paid on the PAYE scheme, and it is simple for them to examine the financial affairs of a registered company. It is now illegal for you to work through an agency as a sole trader, as the result of the 1988 Finance Act.

Turnover is such that many of these companies need to register for VAT. This does offer you the benefit of allowing you to offset the VAT element of your purchases against that charged on your fees. The recommendation is that the company is always registered for VAT. Personal remuneration is usually taken as a mixture of salary and dividends, the exact

> "The most fundamental piece of advice that I can give you is to get a good accountant, who understands the way computer contractors work."

split depending on your personal circumstances.

The most fundamental piece of advice that I can give you is to get a good accountant, who understands the way computer contractors work. You can pay the accountant to do the bookkeeping work, tax, National Insurance and VAT administration for you (for which you will pay), or use one of the many excellent PC packages available and do it yourself. This will take 2 or 3 hours a month, but you will benefit from familiarising yourself with the world of finance. The requirement for a Chartered Accountant to perform an annual audit on the company was removed several years ago for small companies. However, when you start out as a contractor, having several sets of audited accounts for the first few years can help with getting a mortgage, should you require one after going freelance. An important aspect to bear in mind is that the accountant merely sells advice; you are legally responsible for your actions in this field. Joining a contractors' organisation, such as the Independent Computer Contractors Specialist Group of the BCS, can be very useful for learning the ropes.

Afterword

The only thing still missing is a trendy buzzword for the role that we play in the profession. Perhaps we ought to start talking about OOS ('Object-Oriented Staffing')?

current issues

E-commerce is here to stay

It is generally very unwise to make predictions about the widespread adoption of new ways of working and new patterns of behaviour based on new technology. But now the basic infrastructure is in place and the use ($350bn of Internet commerce expected in 2000) continues to grow exponentially, the whole process seems unstoppable.

The 1990s will probably be remembered, in information technology terms, as the period when large-scale growth in telecommunications began. A combination of interacting factors have given rise to this: the changing regulatory framework together with a greater commercial liberalisation and significant developments of technology, including optical fibres, microprocessors and wireless communication. These developments have enabled considerable growth in global trade which has in turn created a greater demand on the infrastructure.

The ease and rapidity of communication which has accompanied this growth enables people to both conduct their day-to-day business more rapidly and efficiently and to consider doing things that were previously inconceivable. It is now possible, and often happens, to place an order for goods today and take delivery at the other end of the country tomorrow – a delay which is due solely to the constraints of physical transport, all other aspects of the transaction having been reduced to a few seconds. It is possible to purchase 'soft' items such as a musi-

Ian Jones

Ian Jones is the Publishing Manager at The British Computer Society where he has responsibilities for all publishing activity for the UK's leading professional IT body. The BCS publishes a variety of magazines, academic peer review journals, books and reports – increasingly the Web has been integrated across the portfolio in a mixture of print and electronic titles. Ian's 10 years at the BCS were punctuated by a 3-year spell at Future Publishing in Bath where he published a number of computer books including the UK's first Internet book series, .net guides.

cal recording without even this delay. A digital version of the recording can be transmitted over a communication link in seconds or minutes.

There is expected to be both the capability and desire to conduct more and more business in this way. A particularly important component of this entire scenario is the Internet and its associated features such as the World Wide Web (WWW).

The Internet is the fundamental structure on which e-commerce is based and the World Wide Web the interface which makes it practical. The Internet is global in its reach and this, together with the fact that the technology provides a new way to carry out business, brings a range of new challenges which must be, and are being, overcome in order that the

> "$350bn of Internet commerce expected in 2000"

commercial benefits can be maximised. These include:

- effective marketing via the WWW;
- knowing who you are doing business with;
- making payments electronically;
- collecting taxes;
- managing without people;
- exploiting the global market;
- handling global competition.

Each of these is a significant area in its own right which highlights major concerns for businesses, regulators and consumers. In addition, encryption techniques – which provide many of the solutions to problems of confidentiality and integrity of data which are essential for proof of identity and security of payment – give rise to concerns for law enforcement agencies. These techniques can be used for secure communications between law breakers as well as in legitimate business.

As a consequence, because e-commerce is perceived to be so important for future competitiveness and because it gives rise to such a special set of problems, there is an enormous amount of discussion on all aspects of it. The UK government issued a consultation document on aspects of e-commerce in February 1999 and continues to digest the response.

At the same time it is unclear which aspects of e-commerce will be adopted and which will fail. In the early days (3 years ago!) there was much talk of selling publications, in electronic form, over the Web. It was suggested that users would make micro-payments – by means of some form of electronic cash – for access to selected parts of a publication on an as-required basis. This sounds sensible and is technologically feasible but there is not much evidence that it is happening. On the other hand Amazon.com has become one of the world's leading printed book

distributors using the Web as its sole marketing tool.

There is no doubt that e-commerce is seen at its best when it is selling goods and services that can be marketed, ordered, paid for and delivered over the Web with no human intervention. The number of transactions that fall within this definition is clearly limited and wider use cannot be managed without human intervention. This might be in the delivery of physical goods or in the provision of advice. It is difficult to develop systems which are clever enough to handle the varied situations that arise in everyday business transactions. For that reason the continuing growth of e-commerce is likely to involve use of the Web to explore and examine options followed by a more conventional process to handle the trickier aspects of the business relationship.

So what exactly is e-commerce?

Simply it is commercial activity conducted over telecommunications networks, specifically the Internet, for data exchange. It should not be confused with other forms of remote transactions like ordering a taxi or pizza over the telephone, paying by credit card for theatre tickets over the telephone or paying by smartcard.

The extent to which networks can help in the running of businesses depends on the nature of the business. For example, the technology is of little help to a nurse during the performance of her primary activity of caring for a sick patient. Jobs such as this where the service needs to be delivered personally cannot easily be replaced by Internet technology, although it might provide a valuable ancillary support for certain aspects. On the other hand a service such as the provision of train or bus timetable information might be done exclusively over a network with minimal human involvement – at least at the point of service delivery. Other activities will fall within the spectrum spanned by these extremes.

In its broad definition, e-commerce has been going on for many years through dedicated connections and dial-up links. The Internet is 'only' special because it is a universal standard that is outside, and bigger than, any particular vested interest (commercial, government or pressure group) and because the cost thresholds for supplier and user are incredibly low.

How can we use e-commerce?

Many of the processes required for the efficient running of any business can be helped by the use of the Internet and e-commerce:

- Marketing can be supported by a well-designed and well-maintained presence on the WWW.
- Communications with customers, suppliers and staff can be greatly facilitated by the use of Web pages, e-mail and now even more advanced systems integration replacing traditional electronic data interchange (EDI).
- Orders can be placed and accepted electronically.
- Payments can be made.

- In some cases the product or service can be delivered over the network.
- New customers can be reached in other countries.

But, this new way of doing business brings with it fresh challenges which need to be addressed:

- How do you prove the identity of the parties concerned in a business transaction?
- How can financial data be exchanged securely?
- There are legal concerns related to contracts, Intellectual Property Rights (IPR) and other matters.
- There are regulatory issues related to taxation and other matters.
- Businesses must put significant effort into maintaining their e-commerce systems. This will become a major draw on resources but is vitally important since the Web site, if there is one, will be the first point of contact with the customer.

"Many of the leading business analysts agree on the predictions that e-business will account for up to 10% of the world's consumer sales within the next 10 years."

How important is e-commerce trading in the global context?

Many of the leading business analysts agree on the predictions that e-business will account for up to 10% of the world's consumer sales within the next 10 years. Most organisations have extended their business strategies to embrace e-commerce, and increasingly some are developing a sole e-commerce business strategy.

Market research has shown that a large percentage of companies are likely to use Internet-based selling within the next 2 years. The panel opposite indicates just some of the current projections which illustrate the importance of e-commerce to the global economy.

There are many challenges facing IT professionals over the next 10 years as a direct consequence of e-commerce. Undoubtedly, there are many technological issues around data integrity and security, which need to be overcome to help combat the resistance and fears of the general public. The business community will also face some major challenges in addressing the way in which they conduct their business.

Above all, e-commerce is here to stay.

In summary the major potential benefits are:

- ability to reach global markets;
- rapidly growing audiences;
- ability to reach varying consumer profiles;
- increased sales;
- increased profit ratios of whole operation;
- provide an edge over competitors;
- cost savings;
- shortened supply chains;
- faster communications;
- enhanced access to information and knowledge.

Business Standards for e-commerce

The European parliament has now agreed a set of Business Standards for businesses trading over the Internet. These are currently under consideration by EU member countries, with the ultimate aim that they will be converted into national law in the respective territories.

In particular the EU directive states that companies trading through e-commerce must have very clear and legitimate business practices, providing public information about addresses and owners. EU countries will be encouraged to develop online dispute settlement services to provide fast redress and customer confidence.

The ultimate aim of the directive is to protect the consumer and help boost public confidence in e-commerce.

Revenues generated by commercial Web sites:
- Internet commerce will exceed US$350 billion in 2000.

European Internet commerce estimates are £18–22 billion by 2001:
- UK £5–6 billion
- Germany £6–7 billion
- France £3–4 billion
- Rest of Europe £4–5 billion

Adult users purchasing on the Web:
- 1996: 29% of adult Internet users bought goods.
- 1997: 40% of adult Internet users bought goods (approximately 2.7 million people worldwide)

Results of Yahoo! European Survey – in May '97. (Yahoo! Europe polled 12,394 users):
- 23% of users in France are willing to purchase products on the Web;
- 38% of users in the UK are willing to purchase products on the Web;
- 39% of users in Germany are willing to purchase products on the Web.

What skills? What rewards?

IT recruitment moves at warp speed. What's hot one minute is on the Arctic tundra the next. So while industry experts agree that the hottest skill to have on a CV at present is Java and HTML, who is to say if this will be the case in a year or even 6 months' time?

Despite this uncertainty there are skills that will always be of use. The Institute for Employment Studies recently surveyed employers to establish the core skills they look for. Their research showed that communication, numeracy, teamwork and problem-solving skills as well as a desire to improve one's learning and performance are all viewed as marks of employability.

They also noted that a third of employers complain that graduates lack business awareness and communication skills. Therefore a successful graduate must be focused on people to stay afloat: gone are the days when the IT department was run by 'techno geeks' who spent hours pondering the merits of obscure programming languages while believing that the meaning of life was 42. As Wilf Voss, until recently the BCS Young Professionals Group officer, put it, 'The people required in the IT industry are gradually changing from those who have a mainly technical knowledge to those who also have a sound understanding of business.' You have been warned.

First steps

So what are just a few of the many jobs available? And what skills do these jobs

> "communication, numeracy, teamwork and problem-solving skills ... are viewed as marks of employability."

James Hickson

James Hickson is 23 years old and is in the final year of a Computer Science degree at Greenwich University. While studying he has been working as the IT Manager for The Blackheath Hospital where he has overseen the year 2000 project and is currently developing the hospital's IT support and strategy function. He is also an active member of the BCS serving on the Young Professionals Group national committee and writing for the *Computer Bulletin*.

entail? Generically speaking, software engineers, database administrators, network engineers, IT consultants, IT contractors and sales people, to name but a few of the people who are sought.

Software engineers have varied roles that require the use of technical and analytical skills as well as excellent personal skills. The work covers all aspects of software development, from analysing existing systems to developing, testing and introducing new ones. Entry varies and remuneration is excellent. This path can lead to a career in IT consultancy for the ambitious.

Database administration is Oracle and Informix territory, where salaries of £40,000 or more are common after experience, while graduates can expect to earn around £23,000 to begin with. Graduates who have studied Oracle or Informix as part of their degree course will be at a distinct advantage.

Generally candidates need a high degree of technical skill, while experience in Unix and SQL is advantageous.

There is always a need for network administrators and engineers. Generally graduate salaries are not as high here as in other IT sectors but the work is varied and interesting, with salaries rising in line with experience. It is worth noting that networking is still a skill shortage area, with many experienced engineers preferring to work as contractors where they can earn more. Salaries vary depending on location and job role. Junior network administrators might earn £20,000 after a year, rising to £30,000 after 2 or more years' experience.

Sales is an area where good candidates can earn silly money. The work is stressful and competitive, so only people with drive and ambition need apply. The work varies depending on the company but generally sales includes providing technical advice before and after installation and providing support to the client throughout implementation. Technical and people skills are valuable. Benefits can be tremendous, with some staff, again depending on the company, earning up to £250,000 – of course, don't expect a paycheque of this proportion fresh from university!

A big development in IT employment is the shift from user companies to service suppliers, as companies 'get someone else to do it'. Service suppliers claim to offer better career paths and more variety than IT departments in user companies, because IT is their core activity. Employment with a service supplier will offer variety of work and the opportunity to work in different environments. However, due to the nature of the business experienced professionals tend to be preferred, so this is likely to be a second stage in your career.

The next stage

Self-employed contractors tend to earn more money and suffer less stress than their permanent counterparts, with salaries depending on skills and experience. For example, a recent survey completed by Springdex found that the average weekly salary for an experienced Visual Basic contractor was £1,533 while permanent Visual Basic staff can expect an average of £480 per week. The role of IT contractors varies enormously with salaries reflecting the current skill shortage. Graduates are unlikely to have the experience necessary to be successful in this field but could consider this option after a few years in industry.

Consultancy is another option for the IT graduate. The work is generally varied and usually involves some degree of travel. People skills are paramount with client contact forming an integral part of the job description. Projects tend to be based on business and IT issues which ensure that the work is varied and interesting. However, while salaries are excellent with the top companies paying between £21,000 and £31,000, the hours can be gruelling – upwards of 60-hour weeks are not uncommon. On the positive side though, a recent survey by Jobshark.co.uk found that within 7 to 10 years of starting their careers 69% of IT consultants were earning between £76,000 and £100,000 per year

Help, I'm unsure!

Like many graduates you may be unsure as to the area where you would like to start your career. After all, can you really decide that programming or networking is for you after taking one or two units at university?

Will an employer recognise your skills?

Do not despair, a career within a large

organisation could be for you. While most employers recognise the difficulties faced by graduates, it's the larger organisations that can provide you with an environment and resources to help make your decision. The first step is usually a 'graduate training programme', which provides an insight into the employer and the many options available to its new recruits. From here the newly trained graduate can make an informed choice as to their career path within the company and develop relevant skills. Of course salaries vary but as a general rule of thumb it's the investment banks that have the best financial packages (see key recruiters section towards the end of this publication). Remember though that financial rewards should not be your only incentive. Ensure that the company's culture and people are right for you before applying. After all, well off and unhappy is not a good combination.

Current trends

So what about the market at the moment? With the electronic commerce explosion, growth in interactive television and more recently the advent of WAP (wireless application protocol) technologies, many professionals agree that these areas will continue to grow over the next few years.

The good news for IT graduates though is that salaries in IT have never been better. Salaries continue to rise above inflation due to lack of experienced IT professionals. A recent report by the Association of Graduate Recruiters showed that graduate salaries are predicted to grow by 5.5% this year to a median figure of £17,400. The top 10% of employers pay around £21,000, the bottom 10% pay around £15,400, with the highest salaries being available in London.

We can therefore expect that with greater demand graduates with the right skills will command larger salaries. In 1999 average IT salaries rose by 7% and continue to rise in 2000 – proof indeed that the IT bubble has not burst.

What next?

Having reviewed a few options available to you as an IT graduate what should you do next? Continue to examine the world of opportunity available to you. Company Web sites and IT recruitment fairs are an invaluable resource to help you decide not only the type of position you're after but also the company that best suits your own skills and personality.

Data Protection Act

Introduction

The protection of personal information is a key task which information practitioners must undertake as an essential part of their duties. The aim of this article is to review some of the background to current data protection law and practice, and to indicate the way the subject may develop and extend in the near future.

Background

The development of an effective mechanism for the protection of personal data has been a long and involved process in the UK. This process is only now reaching a level of maturity that matches the importance of data protection to society. As early as the 1970s, there was considerable public concern, both nationally and internationally, that the development of large computer databases would infringe personal freedom. The Younger Committee reported in 1972 a public feeling that new technologies could give organisations an improper level of control over the personal data of individuals. Following a White Paper, the Lindop Committee was established to determine how the requirement for data protection should be determined and codified in the UK context. This work culminated in the passing into law of the Data Protection Act (1984), which formally defined 8 principles for the protection of personal data in the context of automated processing. The 1984 Act enabled the UK to sign the

John Gilbey

John Gilbey BSc (Hons) MBCS is a member of the Data Protection Committee of the British Computer Society. He is the Head of Computing for a UK life science research organisation and is an honorary lecturer in the Department of Computer Science of the University of Wales Aberystwyth – where he lectures on the role of management in computing service provision.

Council of Europe Convention 108 – the first international treaty designed to protect against the misuse of personal data.

It was quickly recognised that the increasing trend towards European harmonisation would provide both opportunities and challenges for data protection, and the European Parliament accepted a common Directive relating to data protection in October 1995. This gave member nations 3 years to bring their legislation into line with the stated requirements of the Directive.

> "new technologies could give organisations an improper level of control over the personal data of individuals"

The new Data Protection Act

After a period of extensive consultation and debate, the UK legislation to implement the Directive came into effect on 1 March 2000. While it bears a family resemblance to the previous Act, there are significant differences which need to be understood – including changes to the data protection principles themselves.

The principles form the effective foundation of current data protection and need to be familiar territory to all members of the information industry:

- Personal data must be obtained lawfully and fairly.
- Personal data shall be obtained only for one or more lawful purposes, and shall not be further processed in a way which conflicts with these purposes.
- Personal data shall be adequate, relevant and not excessive in relation to the purposes for which they are processed.
- Personal data must be accurate and up to date.
- Personal data will not be kept for longer than is required for the purpose for which they were gathered.
- Personal data shall be processed in accordance with the rights of the person to whom the data refers (the 'data subject').
- Appropriate measures will be taken to ensure that no unauthorised or unlawful processing takes place – as well as to ensure data security.
- Personal data must not be transferred out of the European Economic Area unless the destination has an adequate level of data protection.

How much has the law changed?

Anyone familiar with the 1984 Act will recognise the framework of the principles, so how much is actually different in the 1998 Act? In practical terms, the Data Protection Registrar has estimated that compliance with the 1984 Act means that we are 80% of the way towards meeting the requirements of the new Act. The scale of the compliance operation is such, however, that one early estimate suggested that the first-year costs of meeting the 1998 Act could be as high as £1,892 million.

Some changes are of form as well as substance – for example, the nomenclature for many roles and functions has changed. The Data Protection Registrar becomes the Data Protection Commissioner, a Computer Bureau is now a Data Processor, a Data User translates to a Data Controller and the process of Registration becomes Notification. These changes reflect recent changes in technology as well as the convergence of European data protection perspectives. The detailed definitions have also changed; for example, 'processing' means virtually any use of personal data.

Some of the most far-reaching changes have been made in the conditions which apply to sensitive personal data. This category of personal data is defined as that relating to racial or ethnic origin, political opinions, religious or other beliefs, trade union membership, health, sexual life and criminal convictions. There will be few organisations of any size which do not process at least some of these categories of data in respect of their staff, customers or associates.

The widespread use of e-mail and Internet Web services provides an additional area where care needs to be exercised in respect of Data Protection issues, but any collection of personal data needs to be lawful under Schedule 2 of the Act. Data subjects must generally be advised of who is controlling the data being collected, what purposes it is being collected for and any other information necessary to make the processing fair.

Perhaps the greatest impact on UK businesses will be the inclusion of certain manual data systems in the terms of the Act. Data held as part of a 'relevant filing system' are now included in the requirement to meet the data protection principles – even though they are not held electronically. Existing manual data handling systems are allowed a run-in period before full compliance is required, but new structured manual data systems need to comply with the principles from the outset.

Careers and futures

What impact will the new Act, and the change of philosophy it represents, have on the information practitioner? Perhaps the greatest need is for all those involved in information management and information processing to develop and maintain their knowledge and skills in their professional arena. The rate of change, and the potential impact of this change, has never been faster – so the need to keep up to date assumes continually greater importance. If they ever existed, the days when knowledge of your subject was learned once – and not developed – are long gone.

One example of developing career prospects is the new, but as yet not wholly defined, role of Data Protection Supervisor – a new position expected to have an independent audit function in respect of the Data Controller.

In terms of data protection, I believe that today's imperative for the information practitioner is twofold:

Computing practitioners need to understand the information environment in which their organisation operates – both to protect the organisation from unwitting infringement of the changing legislation and to indicate legitimate opportunities for business development which the new technologies offer. This requirement is recognised in the BCS Industry Structure Model.

The second need is equally great, and possibly even more challenging. One of the most important duties of the professional, in any field, is the use of special knowledge and skills to protect society from any misuse of this specialism. Nowhere in the information industry is this need more far reaching than the protection of individual rights from abuse – deliberate or accidental – by the information processing environment of the new knowledge industries. Whatever part of the profession you join, you will have a contribution to make in this vital area.

The Certificate in Data Protection offered by the Information Systems Examination Board offers one pathway for developing your skills in this area – see the BCS Web site (http://www.bcs.org.uk) for details.

In conclusion

I asked Elizabeth France, the UK Data Protection Registrar (now Commissioner), to give her view of the data protection challenges facing the information industry. This was her response:

'Developments in information technology make it ever easier to share, match and amalgamate personal data. The business objective may be better targeting, better service provision and the prevention of fraud but the risk to personal privacy is clear. The challenge to the information profession is to understand that risk; recognise the requirements of data protection law; and promote systems design which enhances privacy while meeting business needs. It can be done.'

There are few parts of the profession that offer a greater, or more critically important, challenge.

Security – a business prerequisite

Introduction

Security has always been an essential part of business systems. Cryptography was used by the ancient Egyptians. On the clay tablets excavated from Babylon there is clear evidence of accounting for transactions and identification marks. The whole structure of Tally sticks was designed to account correctly while limiting the possibility of fraud. The structure of double-entry bookkeeping is designed to make it easy for bookkeepers to find that they have made a mistake.

Business has always needed to:
- preserve the confidentiality for its trade secrets;
- preserve the correctness of the records of the business; and
- protect itself against fraudsters and other criminals.

It is therefore no surprise that in the modern e-commerce systems being built now there remains a need for effective security for all parties to transactions.

What security is needed today?

Building a secure business system, which connects to the Internet and links up widespread physical locations, is an art. It requires a combination of techniques to address the varied threats to the system. These varied techniques can be grouped as follows:

Physical: the protection of equipment, communications lines, records, systems documentation etc from theft, damage or

William List CA hon FBCS

William List CA hon FBCS is an acknowledged worldwide expert on development of secure business systems. He has written and lectured extensively on Security and Audit topics for over 30 years. He is the immediate past Chairman of the British Computer Society's standing security committee.

destruction. The mechanisms used are locks, fireproof safes, physical barriers, physical access limitations and badges, etc;

Communications: the inhibition of tampering with messages in transit between (and sometimes within) physical equipment and providing mechanisms to identify when tampering (or just a failure) has taken place. The mechanisms used are cryptography for confidentiality, and check digits or cryptography to provide a means to detect changes or incompleteness in transmission;

Logical access:
- The ability to specify exactly the access to data or programs permitted to be used by a person or group of people;
- the ability to limit the access to data from programs, to control which programs and/or data are present on a particular piece of equipment;
- specific identification of a person wishing to use the resources, main-

taining confidentiality of the stored data, etc.

The mechanisms used are passwords associated with access tables specifying the limits, cryptography for identification, authorisation for use of programs or data, etc;

Business applications:
* Restricting access to the functionality of the application to those functions necessary to perform business tasks;
* validation of all input and sometimes output;
* confirming that the programs perform the required business functionality at all times, etc.

The mechanisms used are passwords associated with tables to limit access to menu functions, validation tests within programs, thorough testing of business applications on implementation and after changes, etc.

System design: providing:
* sufficient alternate transmission routes to cover in case of equipment failure or denial of service attacks;
* the ability to quickly detect failures in the business process for example not delivering goods as contracted with a customer;
* the ability to find the mistakes in the system or its use on a day-to-day basis, etc.

The mechanisms used are the standard good system design and development methodologies to ensure that all conditions are considered and appropriate action taken.

What standards exist?

The main standards in use in the United Kingdom are:

BS7799
Information security management Part 1: Code of practice for information security management and Part 2: Specification for information security management systems. It is hoped that BS7799 will soon be an ISO standard.

This standard provides guidance for the development of an information security management system from the initial risk analysis through to implementing an effective system to meet the specific needs of a particular organisation.

Common Criteria for Information Technology Security Evaluation
This standard provides a means of specifying security requirements within programs or systems so that they may be formally evaluated. This is in process of becoming an ISO standard (ISO/IEC 15408).

In addition there are many informal or de facto standards implemented within systems; for example, SSL (Secure Socket Layer) and SET (Secure Electronic Transaction) which are used to preserve the confidentiality of credit card transactions.

What are the challenges for the future?

Access to the Internet and the development of e-commerce are the technological advances promised over the next few years. Wireless application protocol (WAP) and broadband will provide Internet access through mobile phones. Digital television is now just beginning to offer Internet and e-mail facilities to all with a television. HM government has embarked on a major project to deliver government services through the Internet to the citizens; for example, this year for the first time it is possible to complete a tax return electronically yourself.

Underlying the ability to implement this vision is the need to ensure that people will be happy to use the technology. To achieve this they will need to be convinced that it works and the risks of being 'ripped off' are at least as low as present systems. This implies both the development of reliable business applications, including the physical delivery mechanisms for goods and services, and an effective security mechanism.

The security mechanisms requiring development include:

- The Public Key Infrastructure for cyptography exists in a number of differing, limited, implementations at present, the best known being PGP.
- A worldwide implementation or effective method of interworking between the extant implementations needs to evolve.
- The evolution of the present laws in all countries to enable electronic business to thrive, to deal with criminals, and to provide cost-effective redress to citizens when their rights are violated.
- The evolution of fully automated mechanisms to help management

comply with their corporate governance responsibilities and to help the external auditors in their public stewardship role.

- The creation of new methods to effectively manage the security functionality within complex, interlocking, worldwide networks.
- The creation of mechanisms to make it much easier for people to find their mistakes in software, or in using systems.

A final word

The huge benefits of the new technologies will only be fully realised if people are happy to use them. This means it is just as important to ensure that, for example: prices quoted for goods are right, goods are delivered, refunds are paid, Web site information is correct, etc as it is to ensure for example: credit card numbers are not stolen, confidentiality of personal data is maintained, accuracy of records are maintained, etc.

Security is everyone's responsibility. This is a worthwhile challenge for you young people setting out to build a better future for yourselves.

> "The huge benefits of the new technologies will only be fully realised if people are happy to use them."

salaries and
career paths

Career prospects and remuneration

Information technology has become an integral part of almost every business in the UK today, and this rise has been so rapid that there are already more jobs than professionals available to fill them. An IDC report estimates that the shortage of IT skills in Western Europe could mean that there are currently as many as 1.6 million empty jobs. It is obvious, therefore, that anybody with the appropriate skills will be offered a wealth of career choices and high salaries.

But what is an IT professional?

The term IT professional encompasses hundreds of specialisms, from the design and programming of computer systems, through testing, maintenance and support; training of users; and software or hardware sales. You might choose to work exclusively with software, hardware, or applications development.

The type of company you could be employed by is as varied as business itself, but the majority of positions are with blue chip companies in the financial services, hi-tech, telecoms and retail sectors.

Key skills

At the moment, certain skills are in particular demand in the industry. The current top five are Windows NT, Oracle, C++, Unix and Visual Basic, so if you are skilled in these areas you will be even more attractive to employers.

Furthermore, the demand for Internet skills including Java, HTML and C++ has increased significantly over the past 6

Laura Chard

Laura Chard is marketing manager for Elan Computing, one of Europe's leading specialist IT recruitment consultancies. The company offers both contract and permanent IT personnel in all technologies and disciplines, providing services to over 900 companies worldwide. Laura Chard joined Elan in 1998 from BT, where she held a number of marketing roles over 8 years.

months, with companies of all sizes looking to build Web development teams or employ individuals to steer the business into cyberspace.

The demand has arisen from e-commerce being accepted as a viable way of doing business, especially now that security issues have been resolved. The larger organisations are also setting up intranets, placing additional strain on the workforce.

However, while there are many candidates, particularly graduates, who have HTML and Java skills, there are few who have actual commercial experience of implementing a company's Internet and e-business strategies. Gaining this experience can have a major effect on your market value.

Requirements for entry into IT careers

The entry level into IT careers is generally a degree, often in Business/Management, any Computing discipline, Engineering,

Mathematics or Sciences, but because of the severe shortage of employees a degree in any subject is frequently accepted. Although a postgraduate qualification is not necessary, an MSc or diploma in IT may be useful if you don't have a background in computing. It is worth noting, too, that with women making up just 15–20% of the IT workforce, employers are currently very keen to recruit more women.

Most major companies today recruit graduate trainees via the 'Milk Round', that is, by touring the universities and encouraging undergraduates to apply for positions. If you haven't yet begun your university course, you might like to investigate sponsorship by such companies, whereby you receive a contribution to your fees in exchange for working at the company during vacations. This guarantees you experience and a job at the end of your course. With or without sponsorship, you can apply for a sandwich course, where your year working in industry will give you the experience to help with your job search on graduation.

Alternatively, once you have your degree you can approach the companies direct, perhaps using national newspapers and the computing press – such as *Computing* and *Computer Weekly* – or via specialist Web sites such as Jobloop (www.jobloop.com) or recruitment agencies such as Elan.

Prospects

The likelihood of promotion within permanent positions depends largely on the employer. Most companies are now realising that, with IT employees in such demand, they must offer good prospects and benefits in order to attract and retain the right staff, which can be very good news for you. It is also important for them to keep staff trained to keep up with the current trends, so once you are in a job you should receive training in all the latest technologies, which will in turn also increase your employability.

However, an increasing number of IT professionals work as freelance contractors, who often work on a project basis for employers. Being a consultant allows you to pick and choose assignments as so many are offered. Salaries tend to be higher, and there is the opportunity to work on a wider range of projects, but there is less job security and you won't have the benefits of paid holiday and company pensions. You will normally need at least 2 years' experience to become a consultant. Additionally, recent legislation introduced by the government affecting self-employed status may deter potential graduates entering this area.

Salaries

Starting salaries for graduates vary across the country. In Scotland, you can expect to earn between £14,000 and £15,000 in your first IT position, rising to around £15–18,000 in the rest of the UK or £18,000–£20,000 in the Republic of Ireland, with the highest salaries of between £18,000 and £24,000 available in London, depending on whether you have an IT-related degree or industry experience gained in placements or sponsorship.

The increasing shortage of IT skills has caused salaries in the industry to increase very quickly. Between 1997 and 1999 the average wage increase for permanent staff was 10%, and 15% for contractors. Wages vary according to the area of the country, as shown in Tables 1 and 2.

Why IT?

In addition to the higher than average earning potential and favourable promotion prospects discussed above, working in IT offers almost endless possibilities for travel around the globe, working with different types of organisation on all kinds of projects. The only limit is your own skill set, and with most companies offering ongoing training there should be no reason for you to fall behind.

Contractor rates:

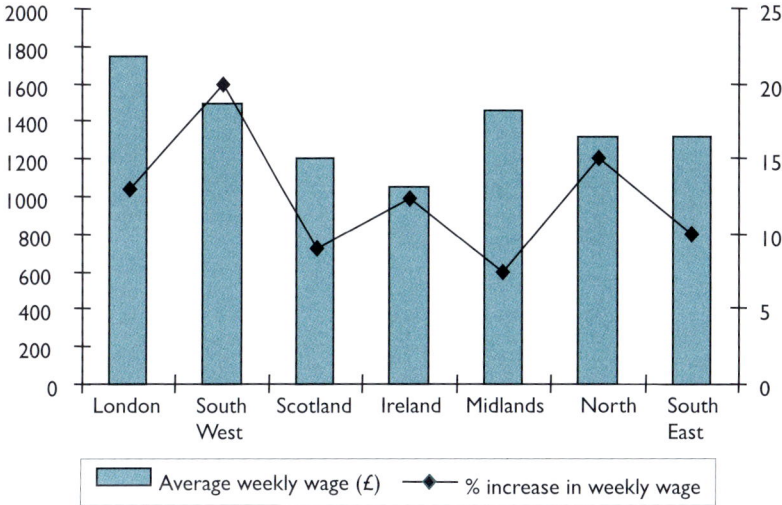

Average weekly wage (£) —◆— % increase in weekly wage

Permanent IT staff rates:

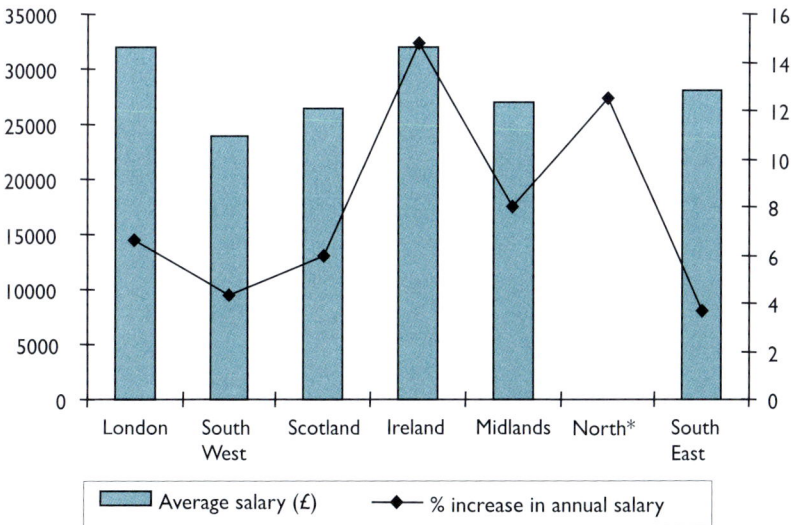

Average salary (£) —◆— % increase in annual salary

(* *salary data not available*)

Where do I go?

If you are keen to take advantage of the opportunities offered by a career in IT, contacting a recruitment consultant such as the one I work for is a sound first move. Consultants will be able to provide personal career guidance, and give you a realistic appraisal of your options, in addition to help with CVs and interviews. Agencies can ensure that you find a job in a company that suits your requirements, skills and personality.

Communications network manager

When people asked me, 'Well, what do you want to do when you leave school?' I just shrugged and said 'Something to do with computers, I think'. I know my answer would never have been 'I want to build and manage the global network for one of the world's leading alcohol companies' but fate has a strange way of leading you down a path, or does it?

Where did I begin?
I left school with a handful of 'O' levels, not enough to step into a decent Information Technology position, but I never gave up on my goal of working with computers. My first position was working in a small independent high street computer shop selling all manner of home computer goods. At the time I know I worried that I was going to be stuck working in a shop for my whole career, but looking back I learned many valuable skills and the ability to work as part of a team. I knew I had to move on and change to a job that brought me closer to the business world of computing. My first move was to that of a computer assistant working within a technical support team within the local council.

I was then lucky to obtain the position of computer operator within a large agricultural company who operated a national network. This position gave me a firm technical grounding for the rest of my career. The role of the computer operator 15 years ago was vastly different to

> **David Keeble**
>
> David Keeble has worked for Bacardi Limited for over 8 years where he holds the position of Communications Network Manager. Stemming from a computer operations background, David has progressed to a position where he is now responsible for the management of a global network spanning over 60 locations worldwide.

how it is today, but many companies required skilled operators to administer and operate their computer systems usually 24 hours per day, 365 days per year in shifts. Any position that exposes you to multiple systems will provide you with choices, choices you can use to guide your career into areas you either feel more skilled at or perhaps those that you feel give the best long-term opportunities. I began to see that the field of networking was an area that I would strive to work towards.

> "I made the decision to leave the UK and work in Bermuda. Actually it wasn't that hard a decision to make!"

My next position was still within computer operations; however, I had made the decision to leave the UK and work in Bermuda. Actually it wasn't that hard a decision to make! I moved to Bermuda to a position at the Bank of Bermuda, again within the Computer Operations department. This position continued to broaden my horizons and my understanding of international business; however, I knew that I needed to move away from computer operations and shift work, and that opportunity came when I was offered the position of Technical Support Programmer working for Bacardi Limited. I seized the opportunity even though I felt I was jumping in at the deep end. I have now been working for Bacardi for over 8 years; during this time I have continued to increase my technical knowledge, and just as importantly, my knowledge of the company. This has resulted in a number of promotions, first to Networks System Manager, where I was responsible for the systems management of all of the head office systems, and then to the position I hold today.

Why me?

My wife always tells me I'm so lucky that I enjoy what I do, and it's true, the role of Communications Network Manager is a position I truly enjoy. That does not mean that it's an easy role, far from it; in fact there are days when I feel the grey hair growing. This is a role that requires good technical knowledge, and excellent people and organisational skills. Bacardi Limited has evolved and grown over the years, and this position was created to support the growing telecommunications needs of the organisation and to implement and position communications technology within the company in a way that supports the strategic direction and various business functions of the group. Before the creation of this position there had been no central communications direction. The initial goals of this role were centred around reviewing the existing global infrastructure. The mid-term (current) goals are to implement a single centrally managed global communications network. The ongoing goals of this role will be to continue to provide a strategic direction for communications technology and to provide proactive network management of the entire global communication infrastructure.

To date I have managed the successful implementation of the global network; this network comprises nearly 40 Frame Relay connections in over 30 countries. Since the implementation of the global network, my role has continued to grow and change. I find more and more that I need to re-evaluate what we are doing in a constant effort to ensure we are making the most effective use of the resources we have available to us. It's very easy to build something, but to allow it to grow and use it effectively, that's what's important. We are currently in the process of building formal research and development procedures to carefully evaluate technologies such as Voice and Video over IP, migration to Windows 2000 and effective use of Virtual Private Networks. Dig the foundation first, then you can build.

If you have chosen a career within Information Technology you will be rewarded with a career full of challenges. The roles that are performed today are forever changing as new systems emerge, I don't think that you will find a position within this industry that will not change, so be prepared to change with it. If, like me, you see networking as a career that you would like to follow, I think you will have a job that will bring new surprises each day; you will need to build constantly on your technical skills and also follow and understand the current trends in technology. No matter how good your technical skills become, you also require good people skills so you will be able to share the knowledge you gain with others.

> "No matter how good your technical skills become, you also require good people skills so you will be able to share the knowledge you gain with others."

Now it's your turn

I often use the analogy of a network being roads; you need to have enough lanes to support the size and volume of vehicles that will drive on it. The roads, like the network, are the infrastructure for business. As you begin your new career journey, think of the knowledge you gain within each job and the goals you set as the infrastructure of your career. I began by saying that perhaps fate leads us down a path, and this may be slightly true; however, you control the direction of your career, so learn, set goals and enjoy what you do.

Project manager

Overview of my current role

As a senior project manager at Quidnunc, my role is to deliver e-business solutions to an extensive portfolio of clients. A successful project is measured in three ways and these objectives drive the role:

1. The project is delivered on schedule and to the agreed cost

An e-business project team will consist not only of technical developers, but artists, implementation designers, branding, strategy, architecture and content experts. It is your job to make sure that the team work closely and effectively in order to meet the project objectives. This incorporates:

- resource management – allocating tasks to individual team members and monitoring progress;
- cost management – knowing the cost position at all times, managing project scope and monthly billing;
- risk management – assessing and managing risk, rerunning the exercise throughout the project;
- quality management – making sure that the solution delivers according to the agreed specification.

2. The client is ecstatic about the solution we have delivered and will allow us to use them as a reference site

Your relationship with a client grows from the first pre-sales meeting. As a project manager you act as lead pre-sales on bids, working closely with the business development team to understand the require-

Patrick Cresswell

Patrick is a senior Project Manager for Quidnunc, an e-commerce consultancy who specialise in working together with clients to define an e-business strategy and then implementing it in interative delivery cycles. Although based in London, Patrick has had the opportunity to travel and work with colleagues from other offices in New York, San Francisco and later this year Berlin and Austin, Texas. Patrick joined Quidnunc as a Project Manager 2 years ago after spending 3 years as a consultant for PA Consulting Group. Before Patrick joined PA he graduated with a First Class BSc (Hons) in Computer Science from University College, London.

ment and shape the best solution for the client. You are also responsible for team resourcing and close liaison with resource managers.

Following commencement of the project you need to build a trusting, professional relationship with senior management in order to ensure project success while also looking toward the future and positioning the next sales opportunity – the next phase.

3. I grow my team and share the knowledge we have gained on the project with our colleagues at Quidnunc

When beginning a new project, you need to understand exactly what each member of the team wants to achieve. This could range from supervising experience through to a deeper understanding of a core technology. Throughout the project life-cycle it is the role of the project manager to ensure that individuals are challenged to allow them to meet their career objectives.

The following qualities are essential:

- Leadership – You start each project with a clean sheet of paper. Starting by shaping the approach in the initial pre-sales meetings to implementation of the e-business strategy in multiple phases. Throughout this it is vital to demonstrate a strong leadership style.
- Excellent communication skills – Whether in a corridor conversation with a team member or presenting to the main board, you need to get your message across in a clear, concise and focused manner.
- Drive and commitment – you are setting the standards for your team and setting standards for drive and commitment, therefore it is essential to lead by example.
- Vision – the ability to keep your sights on the big picture while not losing track of the detail.

Description of how my career has progressed

I always liked the idea of consultancy. Why work for the same company day-in, day-out when you can work for a new company every 6 months and still have the stability of a permanent job and career path? After my degree in Computer Science, a number of my friends became contractors or went into IT support jobs in the City. I wasn't happy with the risks of being a contractor or the limitations of working for just one company, so decided to go into consultancy. Five years on (3 years' management consultancy and 2 years' e-business consultancy at Quidnunc) and I am very happy with my

decision. My CV reads like a who's who in business including clients like Marks & Spencer, Glaxo-Wellcome, ICI Corporate, Deutche Bank, Nomura and Scottish Power.

I made the move from management to e-business consultancy for one reason – responsibility. Working for a big international consultancy, you are one of thousands of consultants and as such it is hard to really make a difference. Key company decisions are made by a select group of 'the great and the good' and responsibility comes with age (and often grey hair!). Joining a company like Quidnunc was a breath of fresh air. When we reinvented from a software consultancy to a 100% e-Business consultancy, the whole company had an opportunity to contribute to how the new company would look. There is an air of openness stemming from the CEO downwards.

For me, however, the most important factor was that Quidnunc reward ability and drive over pure experience and time-serving. As the reward is career development and responsibility (as well as more money of course!) Quidnunc have allowed me to reach a position in 2 years that would have taken over 5 at one of the big consultancies.

How my career is likely to unfold

As you become more senior, you are given the opportunity to manage bigger and more complex projects and one of my personal goals is to lead a market-forming business-to-business opportunity from initial strategy through to implementation. The next major step in my career path is to Principal and from there to Partner where you spend your time building long-term relationships with clients and visioning how the marketplace will grow and where we as a company should sit in this marketplace.

I think that the next few years will be as exciting, as the Internet changes the fundamentals of how businesses operate, as the early years of computing were for those pioneers in Silicon Valley in the 1970s. Be it WAP, Broadband or Interactive TV, wherever technology is driving business change and reshaping marketplaces I want to be involved, and the business understanding I am gaining as a project manager will give me the best possible experience to do just this.

Electronic publishing

Although this article appears in the 'Career path' section of the guide, because changes in electronic publishing happen so fast, it is difficult to identify an obvious career path in electronic publishing. Indeed, even now it is difficult to define the term precisely. However, it is fair to say that it covers all forms of publishing that use electronics and computation in their preparation and delivery. This includes not only the Internet/World Wide Web and CD-ROMs, but also, still, the handling of files that end up as print on paper. Indeed, procedures for producing electronic and what have been called conventional publications are becoming more and more similar.

The other change that has taken place over the past few years has been the growth in importance of computing expertise in effective electronic publishing. What can now be done on the World Wide Web, using progamming languages such as Java and the recently developed coding system called XML (extensible markup language), has changed out of all recognition since the Web was set up in the early 1990s as a vehicle for exchanging research information. And, indeed, the techniques used for providing information are now very similar to those being used in electronic commerce, so that the boundary between electronic publishing and electronic commerce is becoming very blurred, particularly when the latter is concerned with trade in information.

"the boundary between electronic publishing and electronic commerce is becoming very blurred"

David Penfold

David Penfold MBCS CEng is a publishing consultant, editor and writer (EP, multimedia and communications glossary; Review of European Book and Journal Publishing). He is closely involved with the Electronic Publishing Specialist Group of the British Computer Society and is a member of the Society's Publications Board.

The other, very important growth area is computer games. The majority of CD-ROMs now sold are games CDs and this is a large area of opportunity. However, as for electronic publishing in general, a career path is hard to specify.

Where to start

There are very many ways into working in electronic publishing, but this Guide is concerned with IT careers. There are, of course, many computer degree courses in IT-related subjects and there are now also an increasing number of courses related to publishing. The latter almost invariably include modules devoted to electronic publishing, but are also concerned with many other aspects of the traditional publishing industry, so they may not be appropriate if you want to concentrate on electronic publishing. However, there are also many postgraduate courses in areas such as digital imaging and colour reproduction, which will certainly increase your skills in a particular area.

What is important, however, if you want to be involved in the technical side of electronic publishing, is to learn the technical skills and keep up to date. Because the industry is so new, many people have had to learn the skills as they go along, but a solid understanding of the basic principles should not be undervalued.

There are also a number of university and commercial research groups in electronic publishing if you want to be in at the development stage.

What are the skills areas?

One of the exciting aspects of electronic publishing is that the skills areas are changing all the time. Of course, this can be unsettling, but opportunities keep opening up. For example, more and more databases are accessible from the Web. The interfaces to these can involve programming in various languages, such as Java, JavaScript and CGIscript, as well as writing data descriptions using XML and related tools such as RDF (Resource Description Framework), which is all about using metadata (that is, data about data) in order to make finding information a much more structured process.

Another area that is currently developing fast is the use of the Portable Data Format (pdf), usually in the form of Acrobat files, as developed by Adobe. It is in this area that the technical aspects of electronic publishing and what used to be called typesetting are coming together. The same file can now be used either as an electronic publication or as the file sent to a hard-copy imaging device, whether it is a laser printer or an imagesetter. On the other hand, it is a truism to say that so much more can be done in an electronic publication than on the printed page.

Who are the electronic publishers?

Part of the reason that it is difficult to define a career path is that it is almost impossible to produce a profile of a typical electronic publisher. It is only necessary to look at the World Wide Web to see that almost anyone can be an electronic publisher. However, it is also easy to see that there are Web sites and there are high-quality, professional Web sites. What is not so obvious is that the quality of a Web site does not necessarily relate to the size of the organization involved. There are large companies that have poor sites and very small companies that have excellent sites. Many of the most imaginative sites are handled by design agencies, but design agencies that have realized that, while design is important, it is only one aspect of producing a Web site; technical skills are as important, both in terms of planning the site (specification skills) and actually writing the programs to achieve the desired effect.

Of course, traditional publishers are also working in this area, although some are very slow to take up the challenge. A particularly active area is the electronic publishing of academic journals, which overlaps into e-commerce. And, of course, information publishers, such as the publisher of these Guides, are keen to take advantage of the potential of this medium. The main problem that publishers have is not technical, but commercial, in that how electronic publishing can support publishing activities in financial terms is still not at all clear.

Another growth area for electronic publishing is company intranets (an intranet is a network that uses the technology of the Internet, but is private). Many companies are now using intranets as ways of disseminating information internally and it is in their interest that this is done well, so there may be opportunities here, although more probably on a contract basis. While a company may have a webmaster, who will keep the site up to date, it may not need the full-time services of a technical expert.

So how do you proceed?

Although there are well known examples of teenagers producing very successful electronic games programs, in general it is fair to say that, in order to be able to obtain a professional technical position, you need a professional qualification. While this may be a design qualification, a computing or even a specific electronic publishing qualification is likely to be more appropriate. Then, it is a question of looking for opportunities in the kinds of companies discussed above. And, of course, the Web itself is a good place to look for job opportunities!

What is good about electronic publishing is that you do not need to work for a company at all to obtain experience. The cost of setting up your own Web site is really very small and this is a good way to obtain experience. You may even find that if your Web site looks good (and is good), you can persuade a few small businesses to pay you to set up sites for them – and so on! One word of caution, however; what you as a student feel is an exciting site may not be the kind of site that a commercial organization is looking for.

"What is good about electronic publishing is that you do not need to work for a company at all to obtain experience."

Qualities needed

As already noted, this is a fast-growing and fast-changing area. Not everything that develops is successful. So you need to be adaptable and flexible. You need to be able to keep up to date and learn fast. Security may not always be guaranteed, but that is true of many areas today.

In summary, if you find the idea of electronic publishing exciting, and particularly if you would like to combine technical skills with creative or even commercial aspects, then electronic publishing may be for you.

In conclusion

The World Wide Web is now part of everyone's life, directly or not so directly. How this phenomenon, still less than 10 years old, will develop is not clear. What is clear, however, is that the facilities it provides will become more and more powerful, which means more and more complex. In turn, people who understand these complexities will be needed more and more. In one sense, the skills that are required for the successful development of electronic publishing will become the skills that underlie the way that society communicates in the twenty-first century.

IT consultant

Why consultancy?

I was attracted into consultancy for a number of reasons. The main reason was the variety of work it offered. As a consultant you could be working on numerous projects simultaneously. This requires a multitude of skills and experience across a myriad of industry sectors.

Consultancy also provides the opportunity to meet, and work with, a wide variety of people. This requires excellent interpersonal skills and the ability to communicate with people at different levels within an organisation, ranging from junior staff to senior directors. Consultancy is all about working in teams, whether with the client or colleagues. Building, or being part of, a successful team is a key requirement of being a consultant.

Why information security?

Modern business environments are characterised by risk. Organisations define objectives, develop strategies, set targets and budgets, but even the best-laid plans can be shattered by unforeseen events. Organisations are now increasingly reliant on technology, exposing them to increased risk. Unfortunately, the chances of an organisation suffering major disruption to its business are real – apart from genuine mistakes the incidence of organisational fraud, hacking, commercial espionage, system failure and disaster has increased in recent years. There is also pressure on organisations to improve security through increased regulation,

Stuart Anderson

Stuart Anderson, 27, is a Management Consultant with Insight Consulting, a leading provider of independent services in information and communications security, business continuity management and risk management. Stuart has 6 years' experience in IT and holds a MSc in Information Management from Lancaster University. Since joining Insight in 1998, Stuart has performed a gap analysis for a Government Department against BS 7799, the British Standard for Information Security Management, and undertaken a technical security review of the threat to NHSnet, the internal NHS network linking GPs and hospitals. Stuart is currently providing project risk management consultancy for a major financial organisation, working on identifying and managing the risk associated with providing an e-commerce solution.

through the new Data Protection Act, the Financial Services Act and the Turnbull Report, which requires PLCs to embed risk management within their everyday business operations.

The rapid growth of technologies, such as the Internet and e-commerce, and the risks that these technologies introduce make IT security and business continuity a cross-organisational issue with technical and cultural challenges that must be addressed. This, coupled with a technical skills shortage, makes the implementation of secure, robust systems difficult. To overcome these difficulties, more organisations are looking to consultancies to provide the requisite knowledge and skills, and are outsourcing their information security, risk and business continuity management functions to companies such as Insight. The opportunities for career growth within security and business continuity are likely to increase in the future.

Why Insight Consulting?

I was attracted to Insight Consulting as it specialises in security and business continuity and has a blue chip client base. Insight has developed long-term relationships with clients in the financial services, transportation, telecommunications, manufacturing, retail, central and local government, utilities and healthcare sectors. This gives me the opportunity to experience working in different environments with different cultural and technical challenges. Working for Insight I feel I can make a significant contribution to both it and the clients we support.

The working environment

As a consultant, I am working on a combination of long- and short-term projects. I am expected to undertake some of the project work on my own and a high degree of self-motivation is therefore essential. It is important to be disciplined and organised in order to meet a variety of different project deadlines.

To enable me to do this Insight operates a quality management and mentoring system. Insight provides all the facilities required for remote teleworking, enabling me to work from the office, the client's premises or from home. This flexibility makes me more productive and allows me to balance work and home commitments.

The skills

Probably the most important skill in consultancy is the ability to communicate effectively, both verbally and in writing. Findings, conclusions and recommendations must be presented succinctly. Report writing is a major part of the job and the ability to give presentations to large groups of people is essential.

In addition to interpersonal and communication skills, consultants require detailed technical knowledge. Working for a specialist IT consultancy, where clients rely on our expertise, I need knowledge of the security market and products, risk analysis techniques, business continuity management skills and IT expertise, particularly in the areas of Internet security and e-commerce. To meet these needs Insight provides support through training courses, encouraging attendance at conferences and through regular company meetings and focus groups, in order to share 'best practice' and enable consultants to keep up to date with emerging trends.

Consultancy also requires good project management skills. Consultants must be able to manage their time to ensure that objectives are being met in a timely and consistent manner and that the project remains within budget. This requires careful planning and management if unforeseen events affect the project, for example scheduled meetings being cancelled, or illness affecting key staff.

The rewards

Apart from the financial rewards, I thoroughly enjoy my work because of the variety it offers. I also gain immense satisfaction from delivering real solutions to real problems. I enjoy the new challenges and the fact that you are never allowed to rest on your laurels.

The role I undertake constantly changes. One day I could be working for an NHS Trust, helping them secure systems that hold confidential patient data. The next day I could be running a workshop for up to 40 people within a large, multinational plc, focusing on risk management. The diversity of my role, and the associated challenge, is endless.

I believe strongly in working with clients as part of their team, forging long-term relationships that are beneficial to both parties. Having a detailed understanding of a client's business needs means workable solutions are provided, which align with clients' business objectives.

The future

The future? Well, the next step is to become a Senior Consultant. This involves increased project management responsibilities and taking more strategic decisions. I will also be expected to speak at conferences on specialist technical topics, and to liaise with top-level management within client organisations. I will receive continued support and training in order to achieve this goal.

My role will continue to evolve and expand. No two projects are the same so I will be constantly learning new skills and experiencing new environments. I am looking forward to the challenge!

Internet development

How did I start?

With 'A' levels in Maths, Economics and Business Studies, I felt I needed to study a practical course at university, which would contribute directly to a possible career at the end of it all. Although I had never had a real interest in computers for computers' sake, I had always been fascinated by what could be achieved by using the technology in a practical environment. I studied a semi-technical degree course, which combined systems development practices, business techniques and a small amount of programming.

During this time I was introduced to the Internet. In truth, it took me a long time to realise the importance of this technology with regard to systems development and its power as a new medium, as I felt the main application for it was for 'techies' to swap trivia. However, when I joined Publicis, and was introduced to the business applications of the Internet, I became a real convert.

I started looking for jobs before my finals and saw a job advertised in the *Evening Standard* entitled 'Junior Project Manager'. I applied, and after 2 interviews, I was offered the post. I finished my final exam on Friday of one week and started work on Monday of the next.

On a daily basis I could see the Internet becoming a stronger force within the media world and it was obvious it was only a matter of time before it 'took off' and started to affect not only the way we

David Corney

David is the Managing Director of Minerva Systems, a fast-growing Internet development company based in London. Minerva Systems specialise in providing bespoke internet solutions to large and small organisations alike. David spent 3 years working for the Publicis Group, a global advertising and media company, as a project manager/intranet developer, before establishing his own company Minerva Systems in 1998. Before David joined Publicis he graduated with a BSc (Hons) in Business Information Systems from the University of Northumbria at Newcastle.

do business but also how we conducted our day-to-day lives. The Internet was becoming an area that I was not only extremely interested in but also one in which I was rapidly gaining experience.

With this in mind, I decided to establish my own company which would specialise in providing a range of Internet solutions, from the designing of Web pages to provide a basic Web presence for small companies, to developing a corporate Web image with back-end database functionality for larger organisations. After several months of planning and hard toil Minerva Systems was born.

> "when I joined Publicis, and was introduced to the business applications of the Internet, I became a real convert"

A typical day

My team consists of creative guys, Web programmers, marketeers and project managers who usually all play some part in each project we handle.

The day usually begins with a status meeting with the particular project manager for the project being worked on at that time. They will discuss how the project is coming along, whether it is achieving target deadlines and whether there have been any changes made to the functional specification or design brief at the client's request.

At the start of a project the team assigned to it usually meet with the client so that the creatives fully understand the client's preferences in relation to design and the programmers discover the exact functionality that is required. Some clients have very definite ideas of what they require and we very much follow their instructions, and others look to us for advice and expertise and let us run with an idea. Communication skills are vital in this environment as we keep in constant contact with our clients throughout the duration of a project.

The main section of the day will involve the actual development of a site using tools such as HTML, JavaScript, Visual Basic, Illustrator, Photoshop and Flash. The programmers and creatives must also keep in constant contact with each other to ensure that the design and

> "The role of an Internet developer requires commitment and flexibility"

functionality of the site complement each other. It is the project manager's role to oversee all areas and to ensure that the project is running to plan and within budget

The role of an Internet developer requires commitment and flexibility and may require long days and weekends, as deadlines are key. Our working environment is very informal; it's usually casual clothes and the hi-fi playing and that way we are relaxed and ready for what the day throws at us. A typical day in the office is usually from 9.30am to 7pm.

Where to next?

Being self-employed makes the answer to this question rather difficult to answer as it always depends on the success of the business. This is also true for my employees as working for a small/medium-sized business means that their future is naturally entwined with the future success of the company.

Minerva's 3-year strategy is that we will achieve a one million pound turnover by 2001 and establish ourselves as a leading Internet development company. We are on course to achieve both of these targets.

the insiders

Analyst programmer

My plan was always to go to university, but I spotted a local job as a trainee computer programmer that interested me, and despite having no previous experience I was able to get the job and progress to be an analyst programmer. This was made possible through achieving a modern apprenticeship, attending external training courses, day-to-day experience and help from my colleagues.

Monday

There has been a request by a user from our finance department for some new debt-chasing reports. As I currently work on the finance system this task has been assigned to me. I spent some time with my senior colleague reviewing similar reports which already exist, then I ran these reports so I could see the results. I started designing the new reports after studying the specification and reviewing the existing code which I could use for guidance. I still had some questions, so I arranged a meeting with the user. I agreed to complete one of the reports and review it with them before continuing.

I also found time today to produce my monthly report; I do this to update my manager on my progress. Most of the communication between colleagues is informal but we do produce a report to clarify our progress, and raise any issues which we wish to be addressed. I summarise what I have been up to over the past month, listing all the programs I have worked on and what stage they are at; for example, released to live, still waiting to be tested. This month I was able to report some progress towards one of my performance improvement goals. These are targets for personal development

Name: Angela Hembury
Age: 21
Occupation: Analyst Programmer
Qualifications: 'A' levels : Business Studies, French, Biology. Modern Apprenticeship in IT.
Employer: Wincanton Logistics
Location: Wincanton, Somerset
What I enjoy about my job: I enjoy solving problems. In my job they can come in various forms: user queries, system faults and complex coding. It can be very rewarding when you see your programs working and realise how they fit into the whole system, and help users within the business. It can also be interesting and challenging getting involved in new projects and learning to use new software.
What I don't enjoy about my job: I find programming quite frustrating and stressful at times: it requires patience, accuracy and perseverance, especially when working to tight deadlines, and for demanding users. There are also less interesting repetitive tasks such as making a small change to many programs, and system testing.

which we set annually. The goal I have worked towards was to learn a different programming tool that is used in my team. I have completed a small development task using this tool so this will count towards my goal.

Tuesday

An urgent call came from a user based at another site; they were getting an error message which was preventing them from carrying out their monthly payment run. I asked them to give me all the details, but still could not understand why it was happening. I finally remembered to ask a key question: Did it work last time? The user then advised that their PC had crashed earlier when they were running the process. This prompted me to check the temporary files that are created by the process. I was able to do this as it is a network system so I could look at the data they were working on. It was then clear that only half of the data had been updated when the process stopped, so I reversed this by changing the data – with great care! The user was then able to start afresh.

The remainder of the day has been spent coding. Some of the functionality required in the new reports already existed elsewhere, so I was able to use that – no point reinventing the wheel. I did have to create a number of new calculations to organise the figures into the required columns. Also a completely different layout has been requested for the new reports, so that took some time and patience calculating the coordinates to position all the items correctly on the page.

Wednesday

As one of the reports is now complete I demonstrated it to the user, and surprise surprise, they had second thoughts about the layout of the report – so back to the drawing board.

Part way through the morning I was asked to produce an ad hoc report: one of the senior accountants needed some figures reported from the system as soon as possible. Many predefined reports exist for the system but there is always a different combination of data that is not quite covered. The need for us to produce ad hoc reports is fairly rare as some of our users have their own reporting tool so they can create some reports themselves. The larger, more complex reports can be time consuming to create and to run so they are left to the development teams.

Thursday

All the reports are now complete – and in the new layout. The next job was to plan and generate the test data needed to test the reports. I had to spend quite a while inputting invoices onto the test system with particular dates so that I could check the appropriate records are reported in every different scenario.

This afternoon I was called in to my manager's office. I didn't know what it could be about – but it turned out to be good news – I think! I was informed that the department is buying a new piece of software, and myself and another colleague are to be the first to be given the opportunity to receive training and start using the software. We will be sent on a 3-day external course and when we return we will start working on a project, which is now quite urgent, as the waiting list for the course has delayed us from starting. The task seems quite daunting at the moment as the software is unfamiliar and the deadline will be quite tight and I will need to liaise with someone whom I don't yet know. On the other hand it should be interesting, challenging and I will have other people to talk to for guidance. It will be a good opportunity for me to do something different.

Friday
I finished testing the reports today, after fixing a couple of small problems and running the tests again. I then completed the necessary documentation, and moved the reports to an intermediate test system where they were checked further by a colleague who signed them off for release to the live system.

This afternoon we had a team meeting. My project team is split into 3 pairs: 2 people working on a vehicle management system, 2 people developing e-commerce solutions, and my mentor and myself working on the finance system. As our team is a development team we also involve a member of the team who supports our systems in the meetings. The meeting gave us a chance to find out what the other members have been up to, and discuss problems, achievements and future plans. We are also informed not only of the progress of other project teams within our IT. department, but on changes within the business areas which we serve.

Project manager

I was always somewhat interested in computers and technology and as with most people of my generation, I spent some of my youth watching *Tomorrow's World* and tapping buttons on my ZX81 to make an 'X' drop down the screen and hit a landing pad at the bottom (we really knew how to have fun!). But my real passion was for writing… so I've taken a slightly unusual route into the world of IT and the Internet, and like most people have ended up doing what I'm doing more by chance and good luck than by good planning!

I left university in 1995 with a BA in English Literature and Language and one in Creative Writing but not much idea of what I wanted to do. I landed myself a contract with a company called ISI – the IT sister to the massive Mars company. I took the job because it had the word editor in it. Unsurprisingly though, the position of 'Technical Editor' turned out to be more technical than editorial. In the 2fi years I spent there I worked with a technical team to convert over 175,000 documents from different formats, often paper-based, into HTML for the Mars intranet and basically analysed and organised all of the information available to Mars employees. Essentially I had become a project manager (without realising it) focusing on knowledge management projects.

Project management seemed the next logical step, so when a position came up at CompuServe (one of AOL UK's Internet brands), I jumped at the chance. I've now been with AOL UK for almost a year and the role has been versatile, challenging, developing and above all, fun.

Typically project managers within AOL UK are communication catalysts,

Name: Jarrod Frye
Age: 29
Occupation: AOL UK Project Manager
Qualifications: BA in English Literature & Language, BA in Creative Writing
Employer: AOL UK
Location: Hammersmith, London
What I enjoy about my job: Lots of people contact, lots of cutting edge technology to play with, never boring.
What I don't enjoy about my job: Due to the nature of the beast sometimes a huge amount of work will create minimal results.

project planners and high-level technical experts. For any given product we will turn the project owner's wishes into tasks that are delegated between the different departments of the company and supervise them through to completion.

I now have a wide remit, working across all of AOL UK's brands and services (AOL, CompuServe, Netscape Online, AOL Instant Messenger and the AOL and CompuServe portals). At the moment I am project managing 'AOL Anywhere'. This is AOL's strategy to make its interactive brands, services and features available to consumers anytime, anywhere across a range of different devices. Through AOL Anywhere, AOL's members, online consumers of its other Web brands, and millions of other consumers will be able to access popular AOL features whenever and wherever they need them, via the PC, television, mobile phone, handheld computer or other personal devices.

9am

I'm in, PC's warmed up, the day starts! I get online straight away and start to plough my way through my e-mail inbox – in danger of overload if not seen to at regular intervals throughout the day, and check my voice mail for messages. Have a quick look at my electronic diary and check my meetings for the day.

9.30am

Everyone is in the office. I grab the opportunity to catch up with the AOL Anywhere Program Director before he gets pulled into meetings, and we have a brief update on how things are progressing. We have a virtual team for the AOL Anywhere project (we pool all the best resources from across all departments), so it's a case of monitoring closely how they are all getting on and chasing down issues immediately. It's basically my job to keep it all on track and on schedule.

10am

AOL Anywhere 'cross functional' meeting: I have called all the members of our virtual team (from content development/technical development / networks / art) together for an update meeting. A few high-level issues arise that we brainstorm until we agree upon a solution and timescales. I note down some lower-level issues to be followed up later on in the day after the meeting – so that we can try to keep to the hour and a half we have.

11.30am

With a 12.00 meeting coming up, I head back to my desk and deal with any urgent, life-threatening e-mails or calls that I've had since 10am and prepare for the meeting by looking over the relevant information.

12pm

'Jarrod, your guests from.. are here'. Cool, I gather any troops needed and go down to collect my guests. Today, we're meeting with one of our mobile Internet partners, but it could be anyone related to the project, from consultants to suppliers to partners.

1pm

Lunch

Very varied, ranges from chucking a disc in the park (throwing a Frisbee), going for a swim in the gym, going down the pub on the less stressful days, or having a sandwich while sitting at my desk / listening into a conference call on busy days. My favourite involves the disc and the pub and lasts the full hour!

2pm

European conference call: In order to check we are all working in harmony across Europe, and are making the most of our international resources, we try to have a conference call at least once a month – a fascinating mixture of politics, brainstorming, problem solving and sorting out the next best time and place (Jamaica, immediately) for a face-to-face or Wireless Summit as they are now known. Unfortunately agendas don't always run in parallel but it's always fun following geese to almost common ground.

🕐 **3pm**

The USA is now awake, so I take the opportunity to put in a call to one of the International Project Managers, based at AOL Inc., in Dulles, Virginia.

🕐 **3.30pm**

A key part of my job is making sure that everybody on the virtual team has what they want when they need it – whether it is information, artwork, an outside resource, whatever. I use this time to chase up on these things and to follow up on the action points from the meeting earlier today. Whether it's updating project plans, getting dates signed off, delegating responsibilities where necessary,

calling suppliers / partners – no detail is too small. I also remind people of deadlines that are imminent and check that they are on track – key to the successful and timely completion of the entire project. I also use this time of the day to keep up to date on the latest developments on mobile communications, ensuring I've got all the latest information on WAP (wireless application protocol), GPRS (general packet radio services), UMTS (universal mobile telecommunications service) and beyond! I read a lot and also gather information from colleagues – the technology floor is a great place for this.

🕐 **7pm**

Done. I usually leave the office around 7pm.

Support: SAP Project Management

🕐 7.15am – Radio drive in

I drive from York to Leeds University listening to Radio 4 news (doom and gloom) and 'Thought for the day'.

🕐 8am – Managing the e-mail deluge

Where have all these e-mails come from? I cleared my inbox last night before I left at 6.00pm. OK. Back to basics, my time management 4-D's: Do it, Delegate it, Dump it or Defer it. Done!

🕐 8.30am – E-mails into action plans

What? Another 5 e-mails have just arrived. Thankfully no obvious fire fighting is required. I reply to Mark, the Systems Applications and Products (SAP) Development Manager. He asks for the status of a School in the Faculty of Arts. A Finance Administrator is asking for background for a SAP meeting with himself and his Head of a central service resource centre. I decide to respond by e-mail but to follow up with a face-to-face meeting. I open, read and digest e-mails. I use the wonderful 'cut and paste' facility to update my individual resource centre plans.

🕐 8.45am – Education management team meeting

Across campus into the rabbit warren of the School of Education: a set of knocked-through old 3-story terraced houses. Up to the second floor and into the conference room. The SAP support team are already tucking into chocolate biscuits and coffee. The Professor (as Head of Education) chairs our second SAP implementation management team

Name: Terence Langdale
Age: 43
Occupation: Project Manager
Qualifications: Associate of the Chartered Institute of Management Accountants (Registered Member In Practice), BSc (Hons) in Computer Science from Lancaster University, Graduate Member of the British Computer Society.
Employer: Prime Systems Development Limited – working with University of Leeds
Location: 65 Mill Lane, Acaster Malbis. York. YO23 2UJ
What I enjoy about my job: The people! Working with people with a 'CAN DO' attitude to plan and deliver a project. Communicating ideas to improve the project delivery and exploring the most effective approach. Meeting people from diverse business backgrounds and personal experiences. Advising management and staff on how best to implement financial systems and how best to use them.
What I don't enjoy about my job: People who generate stress, or who adopt a 'CAN'T DO ... DON'T DO ... WON'T DO' type of attitude.

meeting. We use a well-established project agenda. We consider issues and progress since our last meeting. The main concern is over the logistics of booking 20 Education staff onto our SAP training courses. The meeting is quickly over. I check with the technical support specialist that the digital projector is hooked up to the laptop. Good – my slides look in focus. I chat to management team members, and then sit down to compose myself for my impending presentation.

🕐 10am – Presenting SAP to Education staff

My audience of 30 Education staff filter in. The Professor opens the session welcoming everyone to the SAP launch meeting. Most will be directly affected by the new SAP system. My PowerPoint presentation lasts thirty minutes.

Why did the university choose SAP?
Because SAP, the 4th largest software company in the world, as suppliers of the SAP/R3 Enterprise Resource Planning system, are committing significant research and development to support the University sector.

What opportunities does SAP provide?
University staff will access university-wide information. Staff can reassess current ways of working and compare with commercial best practice as supported by SAP systems.

How successful is the SAP project so far?
SAP Phase 1 Financials and HR systems went live for central staff on 1 April 1999 – a 'big bang' approach to beat the year 2000 bug. Many resource centre staff went live with SAP online reporting.

SAP Phase 2 Sales, Purchasing and Accounting modules already piloted to some of the largest and most complex academic resource centres.

How will SAP be implemented into your resource centre?
The SAP project team act as agents of change. Each university resource centre will implement the new systems alongside university-wide and local strategic change initiatives.

The SAP team apply a proven planned implementation process, which is continuously refined and improved. This includes a post-implementation review to learn lessons.

I give my voice, and the audience's ears, a rest. My colleague Anne, a FAR-accountant (Finance Administration and Reporting), explains the move to better management information. John, our central purchasing guru, champions how SAP can help the University improve its purchasing power.

🕙 10.40am – Any questions?

The formal presentation over, we sit down and face a steady trickle of questions that soon turns into a torrent: How will we process travel claims? Is there a standard form for paper requisitions? Can we still use our existing sales invoicing system? Our panel answers each question raised. After an hour the floodwaters dry up. I canvass opinions on the success of the launch while people gradually disperse. I invite the team to e-mail me with their views on any major points to action.

🕛 12.05pm – A celebration lunch

Back at my workstation, I update my ms-project Education plan. Tomorrow is Saturday – my birthday. The sun is doing its best to shine, and I have a whole two hours before my next meeting. A dozen people turn up to my open invitation to lunch at the local. They are mainly Information Systems Services or Finance staff – most seconded on to the SAP project. A few like myself are career contractors. We studiously try to avoid work-related topics. This too infrequent proper lunch break together provides the chance to form more personal bonds. Inevitably, work being our common thread and lunch nearly over, a few current project issues creep in.

🕐 1.30pm - Environmental concerns

Paper, paper and more paper. I sort through the SAP implementation pack to pull out purchasing-related documents. John, my co-Project Manager sitting next to me – recruited from the School of the Environment – asks how we can reduce our use of paper to preserve the rainforests. We are managing a research graduate for two weeks. We have set his Terms of Reference to review our University SAP project web site. Can we improve our customer focus? The SAP implementation pack represents one immense body of information. We aim to decrease the volume of paper by publishing relevant documents for online access on our SAP Web site. That should please the environmentalists.

🕐 2pm – Purchasing meeting

Across to the Nuffield Institute to discuss 'best practice' purchasing. Tim and John from the University central purchasing office take the lead. The SAP purchasing system can visibly separate the purchasing roles of: requisitioner, purchase orderer, goods receiver, and invoice verifier. But the Head of resource centre and

purchasing team leader must agree roles, match to staff and decide on the end-to-end processes that will work for them. Can existing staff retain local control over purchasing decisions? Will SAP increase the time between raising the request for goods to placing the order? I am at the meeting to ensure concerns are addressed or raised as issues. We aim to provide a consistent message. An option paper, on how purchasing can operate within the Institute, will be presented to the Nuffield management in two weeks time. This now contains a firm recommendation on purchasing roles. If accepted I will be able to plan Nuffield's SAP implementation in earnest.

🕐 3pm – Communication–planning–communication

Returning across campus I chat about how positive the meeting was. At my desk I update my project plans. I select some report views to assess whether any tasks are approaching their best-by date. I clear down and action e-mails, make several telephone calls, and touch base with members of our SAP support team.

🕐 4pm – Planning and reporting

Time marches relentlessly on. Next week the SAP project steering group will meet again. Steering group members require a resource centre progress update on an exception 'issues' basis. I immerse myself in the challenging mental discipline of progress tracking, making visible issues, and planning. Turning business meetings and action points into meaningful project activities and tasks – discrete resourced time-based pieces of work. My time horizon covers the past week, next week, and key activities for the next monthly reporting period. I update a slide 'SAP phase 2 key milestones' in

PowerPoint. This timeline shows every resource centre's intended go-live date by calendar month.

🕐 5pm – Prepare to switch off

Before I feel able to switch off my PC, I update my electronic diary for tomorrow: more meetings to prepare for, more priorities to set. There we are, all my e-mails sorted. It is amazing what you can carry around in your head. But to assure a good night's sleep, and to ensure continuity in the event of the unexpected, make a note, make it visible.

🕐 5.30pm – Another day over – another challenge in prospect

I jump into my car and switch into drive-mode – a 45-minute cool down period listening to bright and light Radio 2. I arrive back home to the chaotic feeding frenzy of my two toddler sons. At least I have a positive co-Project Manger for support – my GP wife. Another day not quite to plan – but almost!

My background

My 20-year career profile reflects an increasingly common move towards a hybrid finance and IT professional, as follows:

- I am currently working with the University of Leeds, as one of 2 project managers, to support the roll-out of SAP R/3 to the university's resource centres (schools and service areas) this year.
- My previous employers/clients provided the experience of working within volatile organisational struc-ture, business activities and support systems. Organisations include Croda Oleochemicals plc, Samuel Smith's Old Brewery, United Kingdom Atomic Energy Authority, CEGB privatised into National Power plc, Halifax Building Society move to Halifax plc, Richmondshire District Council, British Airways plc.
- I began my career leaving school after 'A' levels in the mid-1970s and trained as a management accountant.
- I completed my CIMA professional qualification, and in the mid-80's moved into systems and business process analysis as an internal computer auditor. To supplement my practical experience I studied 3 degree-level units with the Open University – Mathematics, Organisation and Systems Thinking, and Computing and Computers.
- A thirst for knowledge led me to a 3 year career sabbatical. I completed a full-time degree in Computer Science (2.1) with Lancaster University in 1990. I chose this course based on the department's reputation, and the fact that I was able to construct a modular business-relevant profile accredited by the BCS.
- In the past 10 years, I have specialised in large financial systems development projects in team leader or project manager roles.
- For the past 6 years I have offered my delivery experience as a CIMA Member In Practice: http://www.cima.org.uk/mbr/mip_directory.htm.

Software developer

How I got started

Like many people who work in the software industry, I became interested in computing while doing a degree in an entirely different field. In my case I was working on my Psychology thesis which involved quite a bit of computing. One of the great things about the software industry is that your academic qualifications don't matter all that much – if you have an aptitude for it and can do the job, that's what really counts. I joined IBM as a trainee applications programmer, working on internal IT systems, mainly to do with distribution and warehousing. What I really wanted to do, though, was work on product development. I eventually moved to IBM's development laboratory at Hursley Park, near Winchester. This is IBM's biggest lab outside North America, set in rolling Hampshire countryside, with more than 2,500 people on site. We develop technologies and products for the worldwide marketplace and it's an exciting place to work. I'm currently working on a joint project with Sun Microsystems in California, developing extensions to Java, the new Internet-based programming language.

Name: Larry Porter
Age: 47
Occupation: Senior Software Developer
Qualifications: BSc in Psychology from Durham University, BA in General Arts from the Open University, DPhil in Cognitive Psychology from Oxford University. Fellow of the British Computer Society.
Employer: IBM United Kingdom Limited
Location: Hursley Park, Winchester, England
What I like about my job: Being on the leading edge of new technologies. Travel.
What I dislike about my job: Project administration tasks.

A typical day – Tuesday

7am – Morning run

I start the day with a run in the New Forest. I'm a keen runner and cyclist and like to get my priorities right. So this comes first. I often reflect on my luck in being able to live in this beautiful part of the world and still have a high-tech job. There aren't many opportunities to do this outside the USA.

8.45am – Check e-mail from home

After breakfast I log in from home and check my e-mail that's come in overnight, mainly from the USA and Japan. My product is currently in Beta, which means that it's not yet finished but a trial version can be downloaded from the Internet. There are a few smart people using it and they're finding some problems we hadn't envisaged. I respond to a couple of the easy queries and leave some thorny ones to look at later.

9.30am – Journey to work

After doing some chores at home and putting a canoe on top of my car, I finally set out for work. It's a pleasant 25-minute drive and an opportunity to review what I'll be doing today. Working hours at the IBM labs are very flexible. Since many of us work closely with developers in the USA, it makes sense to start and finish a bit later.

10am – Programming

I'm at my best in the mornings so usually try to do creative things first – writing, design or programming work. Today is a fun activity, developing some sample programs so that programmers can see how to use our product. Being fairly senior, I don't get as much chance to do as much real programming as I would like. I tend to spend more time on architecture, planning and design. I still get a buzz from programming, so this is a treat for me. Back when I was a trainee programmer, I couldn't believe that people would pay you to do this stuff!

"Being fairly senior, I don't get as much chance to do as much real programming as I would like."

12pm – Lunch

I usually take 20 minutes for lunch in the cafeteria. Occasionally, when we have something to celebrate, I'll have a longer lunch in Hursley's club house by the sports ground or at the local village pub.

12.30pm – E-mail

Back to the e-mail. I spend some time investigating a strange problem reported by a customer in the USA and finally decide that it's a bug in our product. I raise a problem report – one of those necessary but tedious jobs I don't like. I send a reply to the customer confirming that it's a defect and suggesting a 'workaround' in the meantime.

1.30pm – Patent evaluation meeting

Last year I was appointed an IBM 'Master Inventor', because I've filed a substantial number of patents over the years. This means that I'm often asked to evaluate inventions by my colleagues, to decide whether they should be formally submitted to the Patent authorities. Quite often the inventors are from other countries but today it's from a young developer here at Hursley. It's his first submission and so my objective is not just to evaluate the invention but to make sure that, whatever the outcome of the evaluation, he is encouraged to keep trying to invent things. The meeting is attended by myself, a patent attorney and the inventor. The idea is a great one technically but there are lots of other questions to consider. Will this invention be important in the marketplace? If granted, would the patent be enforceable? We finally decide that the invention has merit and we will submit the patent. The developer is pleased – he will get a cash award, with the potential for more if the patent is granted.

2.30pm – Design meeting

This is a small meeting with a couple of other developers to agree the design proposal for a component of our product which needs to be improved, based on the feedback we've had from customers. We brainstorm, argue and discuss and finally come up with an outline design proposal. The developer responsible for that part of the system undertakes to write up the design in more detail and get a working prototype by next week.

3.30pm – Documentation

I draft up the documentation which will explain to customers how they will use my sample program. This will eventually be rewritten by a technical writer, but I always like to do the first draft to make sure it is technically accurate.

4.30pm – Travel arrangements

I contact the IBM travel centre to book flights to Toronto for a trip in 2 weeks' time. I'll be talking at the 'World Wide Web 8' conference about the product I'm helping to develop.

5pm – Team meeting

My project is worked on by developers from two companies (IBM and Sun) spread over 5 locations and 4 different time zones. Every Tuesday we meet by telephone on a conference call for over 20 people. We discuss the status of the project, the issues and concerns we are facing and agree the actions to be taken.

> "I'll be talking at the 'World Wide Web 8' conference about the product I'm helping to develop."

7pm – Canoeing

I drive to the coast and meet up with other members of the local canoe club. Paddle sport is one of my passions, including white water, but this evening it's a short, gentle paddle up the estuary for a meal in a waterside pub on the River Hamble.

9.30pm – Conference call and e-mail

Home just in time to join a conference call with colleagues in another US lab. Their product is dependent on ours and they want to be sure that we've met their requirements. Unfortunately there hasn't been time to do all they want so we negotiate a workable compromise. The meeting concludes with agreement on all the topics except one. This will be referred to our management for resolution. Luckily, IBM pays for my second phone line at home so evening conference calls aren't a problem. A final bash at the e-mail and time for bed.

Where next?

I have no idea. We live in a world of fast-changing technology and working in a high-tech company, I can't predict what the exact nature of my next project will be. But I'm pretty sure I'll be working on Internet-related software of some kind. Software is changing the world. Many of the social changes we will see over the next few decades will be mediated by new software, and in particular Internet software. Shaping and building this leading-edge software is an exciting place to be. I can't see me wanting to do anything different.

education, training
& development

cation, training & development education, training & development education, training & development education, training & develop

Routes into the profession and educational requirements

Information Technology is a young discipline and has not really developed a single recognised career route in the way that, for example, medicine, accountancy and law have. Information Technology is increasingly being called Information and Communications Technology (ICT) but we have retained the term IT in this section of the Guide.

There are several entry points. There are also opportunities to progress a career, if in employment, through part-time education and training, or taking time out to study full-time.

About half of the people employed in IT are graduates, with a first or higher degree. Many IT practitioners have transferred to IT from other departments within their company. Others entered after taking a training course, or a modern apprenticeship, an HND, 'A' levels or GCSEs.

Qualifications by themselves do not guarantee success. For a career in IT at all levels effort, enthusiasm, reliability,

Aline Cumming

Aline Cumming is a consultant in IT and Education. She was previously Head of the Education Department at the BCS, responsible for administering accreditation, liaison with the Schools Committee and matters such as collating the BCS response to DfEE consultative papers. Before joining the BCS, she taught mathematics and computing at secondary school, having previously worked in data processing as a computer operator and programmer. Her first post on leaving university was as engineering assistant with British Rail.

achievement and the ability to work with other people in teams are all needed. There is no doubt, however, that a qualification indicates to an employer your commitment and intellectual capability. It provides a foundation on which to build your later career, starting with some seniority.

A university degree becomes particu-

IT practitioners in UK by academic qulaification 1994–98

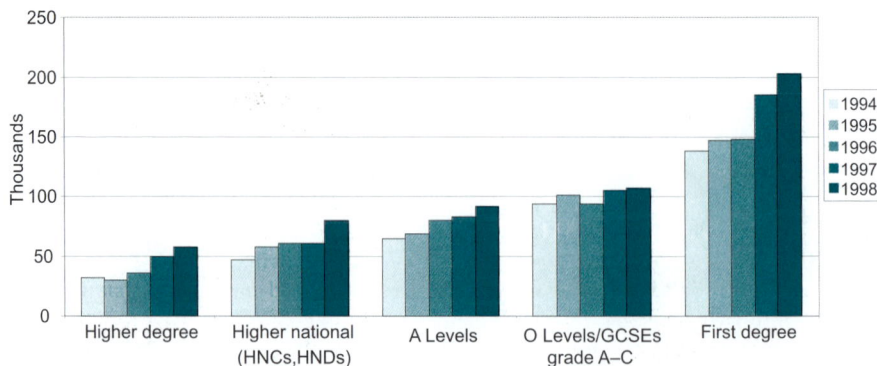

larly important if you are seeking a management position, whether you aspire to managing IT projects or to managing a company. Obtain the best qualifications you can while you are young and education is easily available. When you have a mortgage and children to support, full-time education is something few people are willing to try. Experience and qualifications in management can come later.

The graduate route

You do not have to study IT or computer science for your first degree. Choose the subjects that you feel happy about, although you are advised to keep some numeracy – for example Economics. Many employers prefer to provide training in IT for their graduate staff after recruitment. There are also full-time, part-time and distance learning postgraduate courses in IT open to you, including Open University credits.

The most common pattern for an honours or ordinary degree in England, Wales and Northern Ireland is 3 years of full-time study, which may be with or without a placement (sandwich) year spent in industrial training between the second and final years. In Scotland, where students start after 1 year in the sixth form taking Highers, the ordinary degree will take 3 years, and the fourth year is the honours year; the industry training adds a year to this.

Employers are increasingly interested in the well-rounded graduate, with understanding of the environment in which the computer system will operate. No longer can the elite IT specialist who shuns the rest of an organisation be a prime job candidate. If you do decide to go to university, then consider taking a joint or modular degree. Your experience will be broader than in a single subject degree, although it may prove harder, and you could even include some computing modules. IT is

becoming pan-European: a second language is nowadays a positive discriminator with large employers; there are degrees such as computing and modern languages, or your options in a single honours degree could be in language and European studies. Some employers will sponsor students through their 3 years; others offer sponsorship for the final year after a successful sandwich placement, with or without a guarantee of employment on graduating.

Your primary aim should be to get the best degree you can. Surveys have shown, however, that employers are often more concerned with work experience and extra-curricular activities than degree content, so make sure you have a good spread of interests to offer.

The accredited degree route

The British Computer Society and the Institution of Electrical Engineers both accredit Honours degrees in the IT area for Chartered Engineer (CEng) status. The BCS and the Institution of Incorporated Engineers accredit for Incorporated Engineer (IEng) status, which is more vocational than Chartered Engineer. The Institute for the Management of Information Systems (IMIS) also recognises degrees. Such degrees will have a core of studies seen as the minimum necessary for the foundation of a professional career in the industry, together with a specialist content in one or more areas studied in depth.

There are also 4-year MEng courses in which the fourth year both broadens and deepens the study, which includes more material on management and costing issues. Work experience is gained in vacations. These form the preferred educational element to the route to Chartered Engineer status.

Consider also joint degrees, which may be recognised by the BCS. For the more technical, there are degrees such as computing and electronics, which will probably be accredited and make you eligible for CEng or IEng status. Remember that IT is evolving and developing all the time; degrees are subject to annual review and adaptation and options may open up which are not initially available to you, so keep your eyes open.

The variety of degree and diploma titles reflects the wide choice in the subject-matter of the courses available to choose from. The four major streams under which the subject is presented in the UCAS guide are Computer Science, Computer Systems Engineering, Software Engineering and Artificial Intelligence.

Modular degrees give a wider choice, but such choice may be limited by the need to satisfy the core subjects for accreditation. If you are interested (or think you may be interested in the future) in becoming a Chartered Engineer or Incorporated Engineer, then before you start any degree course, confirm with the University, the BCS or the Engineering Council that your chosen degree is, or is in the process of becoming, accredited by the BCS or the IEE.

To sum up, for Chartered Engineer status the route is MEng (or BEng/BSc plus one year matching section – equivalent to a further year's study), professional development and a professional review interview.

Alternative education routes

A Higher National Diploma or Certificate in subjects such as computing, computer studies, software engineering or business information systems provides a more vocational and less academic orientation than an honours degree. They are technician-level qualifications; an HND may include work experience and an HNC is studied part-time. Some are partially accredited by

the BCS, although a pass degree is the preferred route to IEng status.

Hardware support staff are often recruited from a technical electronic background with an HNC or HND qualification, or a sandwich degree course, as employers tend to ask for experience. GNVQs (GSVQs in Scotland) offer a broad preparation for employment (as well as a path to higher education).

BTEC and SCOTVEC National Certificates and Diplomas are for those who wish to develop their careers in employment from an early stage and there is a BTEC or SCOTVEC First Course in information technology applications.

The training route

This is a popular way to enter IT. A specific training course in a skill which is currently in demand is a quick way to satisfy the ever-growing need for trained staff and to enter the industry. The recent expansion in the Internet and World Wide Web has generated the need for staff who can specify, design and implement Web pages for a wide variety of businesses and organisations, while Enterprise Resource Planning (ERP) skills are in demand not only in manufacturing but also in the financial and personnel sectors.

Organisations such as Microsoft (for Windows), Novell (for networking) and Oracle (for databases) offer certification courses. The Information Systems Examination Board (a BCS subsidiary) offers qualifications in Systems Analysis and Design and Project Management among others. You can attend classes, but the cheaper options are computer-based training or distance learning.

When considering courses, choose carefully, as some short courses in methodologies and specific computer languages are intended for the experienced practitioner and not the beginner.

Make sure that, as a result of your course, you can provide evidence that you have completed some design exercises for someone other than your trainers or your own use. Employers will be reluctant to recruit you unless you can prove that you are competent, not merely that you attended a course and passed at the end of it.

The demand for a particular skill may be short-term so once you have a foot in the door it is wise to broaden your experience as quickly as possible, preferably at your employer's expense of course.

There is doubt, however, in some quarters that a specific skill alone, without the generic skills and background knowledge provided by an educational qualification, give a sound grounding for a career in IT. Professional examinations will supply that grounding, and may be achieved through part-time study. They are offered by both the BCS and the IMIS. The Engineering Council in its examination also offers papers in the IT area. Other bodies offering qualifications accepted by employers are the Association of Computer Professionals, the Institution of Analysts and Programmers, and the Association of Business and Administrative Computing.

Other routes

There is a modern apprenticeship scheme in operation, which runs in conjunction with employers who support employees through IT training and NVQs. These companies recruit from school-leavers, so watch for advertisements for trainees in your local newspapers.

Employers recruit for technician-level jobs in hardware design, testing and development, computer servicing and maintenance, computer operating, sales and customer support, from school-leavers with relevant certificates, at age 16 or 18. A likely starting point is the NCC/City and Guilds Basic Certificate in computer programming, or an RSA certificate.

Large organisations sometimes offer opportunities for their employees to transfer to an IT division within the company. Training, education and experience will come with the package. There are advantages for both employer and employee in this route, so it pays to watch for these chances, with relevant certificates. As a start, the European Computer Driving Licence for the computer user indicates an interest.

The mature student, without qualifications, but with substantial experience and responsibility, can have this recognised under an accreditation of prior learning (APL) scheme. You should consult your local Training and Enterprise Council (TEC) or Local Enterprise Council (LEC). Universities and colleges operate access courses including IT specifically designed for the mature student with neither academic qualifications nor appropriate experience.

Do bear in mind that if you have acquired the skill to design Web pages – not difficult with the software available today – there is a developing market in electronic commerce. It is well worth contacting local companies, who might be grateful to use your knowledge – and, of course, this gives you a foot in the door.

Conclusion

The three elements of education, training and responsible experience are needed to qualify for professional status in IT, computing and information systems, including the engineering core subjects. Evidence of IT training and of seniority can be offered in place of formal education.

The routes to one of the many careers in IT are various, and in the light of the current skills shortage, opportunities abound.

The importance of accredited degrees

The accreditation and exemption process examines courses in the university and college sectors of higher education to see if they are helping to develop graduates who have a professional approach to solving problems within Engineering domains. The academic courses which they are following should contain an appropriate mix of engineering principles, design, professional issues, underpinning theory and practical work.

The British Computer Society (BCS) and the Institution of Electrical Engineers (IEE) have active programmes of accreditation of courses in IT and Information Systems Engineering. Accreditation leads to CEng or IEng status. In addition the BCS recognises courses as giving exemption from its Professional Examination, leading to Associate or full Membership of the Society.

The process

The BCS conducts accreditation exercises by visiting the institution concerned, as well as by means of documentary submission. The visits are necessary because of the need to ascertain the environment and existence of appropriate facilities for the courses. The visiting panel is drawn partly from industry and partly from academic institutions.

Possible outcomes of an accreditation visit include exemption from some or all of the Society's requirements for professional membership, recognition as satisfying the educational requirements for CEng (Chartered Engineer) or IEng

John A McInnes

Dr McInnes CPhys CEng FBCS MInstP is a Senior Lecturer in the Department of Computer Science at the University of Strathclyde, Glasgow. He has been a member of the British Computer Society's Academic Accreditation and Exemptions Committee since 1990 and is currently the Chairman of that Committee.

(Incorporated Engineer) registration, and combinations of the former two scenarios.

The visit

When an accreditation visit takes place, the panel looks, among others, for the following features.

Breadth and depth of coverage

Computing is a broad discipline and no one course can be expected to cover all aspects of it. Nevertheless, courses should provide a reasonably broad treatment of computing. In BCS terms this is measured by whether the course includes sufficient material for exemption from the Society's Certificate and Diploma examinations and from the Professional Project at Diploma level.

A course for which exemption from the Certificate, Diploma and Professioanl Graduate Diploma and the Professional Project at Professional Graduate Diploma level is sought (all honours degrees in computing, and MEngs) should, in addition to the breadth requirement, involve the students in studying in some depth at least one specific area. This depth must be appropriately underpinned by theory.

Professional issues
The BCS has defined the professional issues which it would wish to see in courses (including interpersonal and communication skills, legal issues in computing, and codes of conduct). These should be assessed for, as well as delivered to, all students on the course.

Design
Accredited courses are expected to have a strong emphasis on design, be it systems, software or hardware based on a methodical, structured approach, and involving an appropriate amount of practical work.

Practical work and projects
Practical work, which contributes to the overall assessment, is seen to be an essential component of courses in computing which are preparing the next generation of computing professionals. Any course seeking exemption or accreditation should have a major individual project within it, which gives students experience of a large-scale piece of work, the management of which they have to control themselves. It should involve practical implementation.

The practical work and project must be of a significant scale, reflecting the complexity of real life, and must aid the integration of the various modules of the course. Particular attention is paid to the logistics of practical work, especially with regard to group work.

Engineering principles
The BCS pays particular attention to ensuring that courses have a strong engineering dimension. This involves some of the features already mentioned but also clear evidence of engineering principles and practice and study of the indus-trial/managerial/organisation/economic context is expected to be displayed.

Supervised work experience
Some, but not all, of the courses visited will include supervised work experience. Its value has long been recognised in higher education. It provides an opportunity for students to acquire maturity and certain important knowledge, skills and attitudes which cannot be developed fully within the academic institution. This is invaluable for the prospective employer.

Resources
In addition to aspects of the course design the accreditation process looks at resource issues.

A key resource in any course is the academic staff who teach on that course. They need to be up to date with developments in the industry so that students graduate with a forward-looking approach. This means that staff need to be active in research relevant to the course, and in consultancy or collaboration with industry.

In a computing course with a practical, vocational orientation, hardware and software are clearly critical resources. The students need regular and sufficient access to equipment and software of an appropriate sophistication. The need for good software tools is also of great importance. There is a need for adequate numbers of technical and administrative staff to support the resources.

A good library is another essential tool of the well-educated computer professional. Students should have access to sufficient numbers of appropriate textbooks and relevant journals.

Conclusion
The accreditation process may be considered as an audit vehicle which can give

confidence that an accredited or exempted computing course meets the needs of particular sections of the industry and the Information Systems Engineering profession.

Thus, if you are a student looking for a career in information systems engineering, you should consider a course which has been accredited or exempted by the BCS or IEE; and if you are an employer looking for a graduate with specific skills and knowledge, accredited or exempted courses provide a hallmark of quality.

Graduate training schemes and placements

What kind of schemes are we talking about?

Depending on your age and stage of education, you might consider three kinds of training scheme:

- 'Sandwich' course schemes, which offer undergraduates the opportunity for work placement based experience of 6 or 12 months;
- graduate development schemes offered by employers for new employees wanting to work in IT;
- in-service development programmes for existing graduate staff who wish to transfer to work in Information Systems or need to know more about the area for the effective execution of their principal work.

Which graduates are eligible?

That really depends on the sort of work you seek. Broadly, work in IT/IS may be principally concerned with the technology and the provision of infrastructure, or with the development and implementation of applications and support of people using them.

Graduates wanting to work on the technology and the provision of infrastructure-based services will need a scientific degree, preferably in a related area like Computer Science or Electronic Engineering. Undergraduates seeking work placement in these areas should therefore be studying for a relevant degree.

Graduates working on the development and implementation of computer and network-based applications may come

Geoffrey Mcmullen

Geoff has worked in IT for 37 years. His experience covers everything but hardware design and maintenance. He is CEO of the company responsible for running JANET, and Vice-President Professional Formation of the British Computer Society. He has chaired the University of London Careers Service and the IT National Training Organisation.

from a wider range of backgrounds. Indeed, it is difficult to exclude degrees. Psychology is a useful basis for designing the human–computer interface; Graphic Design can be a good background for Web-related activities; traditionally, Classics is a field whose graduates are trained to think, and many pioneers of computing were from that field. However, the less immediately and obviously relevant your degree to Information Systems, the better the training course will need to be.

Work on technology and infrastructure is clearly an engineering discipline, and you will need a proper engineering formation for it. Systems work is broader in its requirements, more fluid in its application, and open to people from any background. As a career or profession, it is similar to law or accountancy. An intelligent person with a proper training after graduation can do it and succeed.

Sandwich courses

If you are a student considering applying for an undergraduate course, you should remember that computer-related courses are at least in large part vocational. This means that the idea of a sandwich placement makes a great deal of sense. Through it you can develop practical experience in your chosen field and find out whether you really do want to work in it, or which part of it most attracts you. A successful work placement is also a fairly standard channel to employment, which can be an important consideration when jobs are harder to find.

Generally speaking, HE and FE Quality Assurance measures ensure that the learning experience a placement offers will be of suitable quality and relevant and consistent with the aims of your degree. Nevertheless, in choosing such a course, you may find it helpful to ensure that the prospectus offers evidence of success in placing students in suitable work experience areas.

As an example, my own company takes one or two undergraduates from sandwich courses each year and enables them to complete single projects that contribute to the development of our network services. They have the advantage of developing their ability to work in teams in a friendly environment, related to their academic experience as we run the universities' network – JANET. We provide them with a local supervisor and mentor. Their university provides an academic supervisor who visits us to set up the assignment, then visits the undergraduate to check on progress through the year. We get good value; the student develops; and the university is able to offer a broad learning environment, not limited to the classroom and laboratory.

New graduate development programmes

Employers of all sizes in both the supply and consumer side of the IT sector offer graduate development programmes. My own experience was mainly with Shell, where we moved from an entirely internally developed programme to one based on the British Computer Society's Professional Development Scheme (PDS). Whether a scheme is local to the employer or based on some more objective standard like PDS, the key attributes to look for are:

- evidence of genuine managerial commitment to the scheme – does it feature prominently in their brochures, can they speak about it at interview?
- a well-developed description of work in the sector, together with a clear plan for individual progression through various layers of competence and authority;
- a means of keeping the scheme up to date;
- a system for mentoring people in the scheme as they progress;
- a process of salary administration to reward your developing competence and skills on time;
- evidence that successful previous members of the scheme have made good career progress with the employer.

In-service development programmes

Many large companies still run this sort of training programme in IT, but an interest in them implies that by wanting to switch, you have not thought about IT as your first choice of career. Too strong an interest could convince prospective employers that you are indecisive, don't know your own mind and are not a good prospect. However, they're worth mentioning for two reasons:

- As every undergraduate knows, IT is all-pervasive, so it is a good idea to ensure that your prospective employer recognises this fact and is open minded about training employees in all disciplines in effective use of the technology.

- From their attitude in this area, you can get a good idea of their general approach to training. Few employers would now acknowledge a belief that training is an unavoidable but distasteful expense, but many believe it, as is shown by the continuing tendency of companies to cut training investment whenever there is the hint of a recession. Lifelong learning is now a necessity for all of us, because of the rate of change in work. It's better, if you have the choice, to work for a company that sees training and education as a good investment, rather than one that resents it.

BCS Professional Examination

The rapid growth of the IT industry and the rate of technological change within it creates a huge demand for appropriately qualified staff to work in all sections of the industry: in software companies, and in organisations for which IT is essential to business success. The emphasis placed by successive governments on the role of IT in schools and the national curriculum is helping to ensure that future entrants to the job market will have some familiarity with computers and information systems. However, competence in using computers should not be confused with the knowledge and skills required of a computer professional. Furthermore, demand for qualified staff still far outstrips the supply of qualified graduates entering IT careers and there are many people working as computer professionals whose formal qualifications are in other disciplines and whose knowledge and skills in IT have been acquired 'on the job'.

As we enter a new century, public awareness of the need for high-quality, reliable and secure systems is increasing and with it the demand for competent professionals to develop and support them. The professional bodies in the field work actively to ensure that systems development is undertaken by appropriately qualified people, who are able to apply relevant methods and standards and who are aware of legal, social and ethical issues involved in information systems work.

The British Computer Society has, since 1968, run a professional examination

Elizabeth Hull

Professor Elizabeth Hull BSc PhD CEng FBCS is Professor of Computing Science at the University of Ulster. From 1986 to 1996 she was Head of the Department of Computing Science. She has over 20 years of research, teaching and course development experience with particular interest in Software Engineering. She is the author of about 80 published research papers in journals and international conferences and she has been appointed as an external examiner at a range of UK universities. She is currently Chairman of the Professional Examination Board of the British Computer Society and a member of its Professional Formation Board.

in the UK and throughout the world. The BCS Professional Examination sets the standard for professional membership of the British Computer Society and provides a framework against which other qualifications can be assessed. It also offers a route to Membership for people working in Information Systems who, for many reasons, do not possess a formal qualification in the subject. Typically, around 2,000 candidates take the Examination each year.

> "competence in using computers should not be confused with the knowledge and skills required of a computer professional"

Features of the BCS Professional Examination

The BCS Professional Examination is primarily intended for people working in

Information Systems and aims to provide a broad education while allowing candidates to develop depth of knowledge in a more focused area. The emphasis of the examination is on the practical application of knowledge within the workplace, rather than on purely academic issues. For many of the candidates this emphasis on practical applications is attractive, both because it encourages them to make use of their learning experiences at work and because it takes appropriate account of their existing experience and practical skill. To ensure that the BCS Professional Examination is relevant to the needs of Information Systems professionals, the Professional Examination Board, which sets the examination and maintains the syllabus, includes a number of experienced practitioners from various sectors of commerce and industry, as well as experienced academics. The syllabus is reviewed regularly and advice is sought from representatives of the industry about how the syllabus should be developed. The standard of the examination is widely recognised. Most UK universities will accept the examination as an appropriate qualification for entry to degree courses at the appropriate level and in some countries the qualification would allow the holder to be employed in government posts alongside university graduates.

Structure of the examination

The examination consists of three stages, leading to Associate Membership (AMBCS) or full Membership (MBCS) of the British Computer Society, qualifications that are highly regarded by leading

employers around the world. The modular structure is attractive, offering 3 levels of qualification – Certificate, Diploma and Professional Graduate Diploma. This allows candidates to demonstrate their expertise at a chosen level and progress at their own pace. At each level, the Professional Examination syllabus reflects a practical mix of up-to-date theory and current working practice.

Passing the Certificate and Diploma and undertaking a Professional Project at Diploma level, which is equivalent to a Higher National Diploma in the UK, will lead to Associate Membership of the BCS. Full membership is gained by passing the Certificate, Diploma and Professional Graduate Diploma and undertaking a Professional Project at Professional Graduate Diploma level. This is internationally recognised as equivalent to a British Honours Degree.

The BCS aims to ensure that the examination syllabus reflects current practice in the computer industry and the Professional Examination Board reviews the detailed content of all the papers annually. Major reviews of the structure of the examination take place less frequently and these offer the opportunity to consider ways of making the examination more flexible and better suited to the needs of candidates who combine study with a demanding professional career. Recently, this review process has led to a relaxation of the requirement for candidates to have at least a year's experience in information systems work – a move designed to help people seeking to make a career change.

Postgraduate degrees and diplomas

There are various types of postgraduate degrees and diplomas in computing. First, taught courses can be distinguished from degrees by research, though many research degrees have a taught component. Secondly, specialist (or advanced) taught courses can be distinguished from conversion taught courses.

Taught courses

Taught courses are offered as Postgraduate Diplomas or Masters programmes (normally MSc). A Postgraduate Diploma is frequently offered as a subset of an MSc, and can equate to the taught element without the project and dissertation which is necessary for the Masters qualification. Thus a Postgraduate Diploma might be seen as a stepping stone towards an MSc, as a fallback position for someone who, for whatever reason, is unable to complete the MSc, or as a qualification in its own right. Usually the Postgraduate Diploma has a duration of 1 academic year (or equivalent in part-time mode).

An MSc in computing would involve, in addition to the taught programme, a project leading to the writing of a dissertation. This major piece of individual work is expected to involve in the region of 400–500 hours of effort. It should tackle a reasonably complex problem, apply the disciplines of the course, and produce an academically rigorous report. This applies both to conversion and specialist Masters programmes.

Conversion programmes

Conversion Masters courses were initially developed in response to the shortage of

John A McInnes

Dr McInnes CPhys CEng FBCS MInstP is a Senior Lecturer in the Department of Computer Science at the University of Strathclyde, Glasgow. He has been a member of the British Computer Society's Academic Accreditation and Exemptions Committee since 1990 and is currently the Chairman of that Committee.

employees skilled in the use of information systems. Graduates of disciplines other than computing can enter such courses and are 'converted' to computing via an academic programme delivered over 1 calendar year. It is expected that by the end of the course the graduates will be performing at the level of an honours graduate in computing though over a narrower range of material. The courses need to move at a fast pace, since it is assumed that the good honours graduates who enter them have learnt through their first degree how to learn, how to get the most from the teaching and how to manage their time. The subject coverage of conversion courses is necessarily broad, and you will find variation in the focus of particular courses. There are some which are mainly concerned with software engineering, others with systems analysis and design, others with artificial intelligence, others with the hardware side of information systems and so on. You need to look carefully at the particular course to be sure it matches your needs and interests. These courses have been very successful in achieving their purpose and many thousands of graduates have found jobs in computing. Financial support for students wishing to take such courses is available from the Research Councils, the European Social Fund and also from Training and Enterprise Councils (TECs) via the Training for Work programme. You should contact your local TEC or higher education institution for details.

Specialist or advanced programmes

The entry qualification for a specialist or advanced Masters course is a good honours degree in computing or a closely related discipline. Such taught courses are designed to build on the first degree by taking the student to a greater depth in a narrower area of the discipline. Courses might focus, for example, on human–computer interaction, or robotics, or distributed systems. The expectation is that the student will have already studied at honours level in the area which is to be pursued in greater depth. There are far fewer places on specialist or advanced MSc courses. Funding may be available from the Research Councils via the universities, though some employers sponsor graduates on such courses.

Continuing Professional Development

Increasing use is being made of postgraduate courses/modules for professional updating as part of Continuing Professional Development schemes. These can be at conversion or specialist levels. Regular updating of skills is an essential requirement for the Information Systems Engineering professional and courses/modules at postgraduate level are a good way of meeting these requirements. Modules may be offered as blocks (involving a period of study at the university preceded by pre-course reading and

followed by an assessment in some form) or over a semester of 12–15 weeks on a part-time basis. It is possible through credit accumulation and transfer schemes to gain credit towards a qualification via these modules.

Professional accreditation of taught postgraduate courses

The British Computer Society maintains a list of approved postgraduate programmes. Appropriate conversion courses can be approved for exemption from Diploma level of the Society's examinations and from the Professional Project at Diploma level. This provides a route to full professional membership, after suitable experience and training, for honours graduates of disciplines other than computing. In order to receive approval for exemption at Diploma level, courses will be examined to ensure that they offer sufficient breadth of study, significant practical work, treatment of professional issues, and an emphasis on engineering principles, especially design. Specialist or advanced courses can be approved for exemption from Graduate Diploma level of the Society's examinations and from the Professional Project at Graduate Diploma level. Usually this is not particularly relevant to the graduates because in most cases they will already be exempted from the Diploma and Graduate Diploma levels and the Professional Project at the Graduate Diploma level on entry by virtue of their first degree in computing. However, it can be useful for those who enter with only a Diploma level exempting qualification. The main reason to look for a course which has been approved by the BCS is that it will have been checked for its depth, its coherence, its engineering emphasis, the nature of its practical and project work and the resources available to support the programme.

Appropriate courses may also be recognised as satisfying the academic requirements for registration as an IEng (Incorporated Engineer).

Degrees by research

The main degrees by research are MPhil and DPhil or PhD, although some institutions offer a research MSc. Applicants need to have a good first degree in computing or a closely related discipline. There are not very many funded research studentships available and so the competition is fierce. Most candidates register at first for an MPhil, and transfer after about 2 years to a PhD if the research looks as though it will reach a sufficiently innovative level. The expected period for a PhD is 3 years full-time; usually this period should include the writing of the thesis. Research students, for whom the research for the degree is the main focus of activity, are funded by a grant (often called a bursary), whereas research assistants, who are assisting in research on a particular project, are paid a salary. In either case the researcher should have a director of studies and one or more supervisors who will help to provide guidance and direction for the research. The researcher often has to have strong self-motivation and to explore ideas of his or her own. Increasingly universities are expected to provide some training in research for research students and assistants. Research in computing is very wide-ranging because of the continually expanding areas of application of computers. A good place for prospective postgraduate students to start with preliminary enquiries is the academic staff at their university during their first degree.

Continuing professional development

Introduction

All professional institutions require their members to participate in Continuing Professional Development (CPD) in order to maintain and enhance their skills.

The Engineering Council defined Continuing Professional Development as:

'The systematic maintenance, improving and broadening of knowledge and skill and the development of personal qualities necessary for the execution of professional and technical duties throughout the individual's working life.'

Continuing employability is dependent on maintaining and developing your skills.

It is absolutely essential that you take control of your technical and professional development, decide your objectives, and plan your learning to meet your needs. All learning situations are relevant; the more focused the learning is to your objectives the greater its value. The better employers will provide advice and guidance on career development; however, training provided when it is beneficial for the company may not be so forthcoming when it is not relevant to your current work. Developing and executing your plan is your Continuous Professional Development; this is the best way to maintain continuous employability.

CPD and professional societies

Institutions where the work is safety critical, such as medical, lay down stringent rules regarding CPD for their members to be allowed to practise. Others such as

John Gardner

John Gardner, Ceng, MBCS, MIMIS, AMIEE, is the Chairman of the BCS Working Party for CPD. Following 7 years' research work in electronics he has over 35 years' experience in all aspects of computing, with computer manufacturers, software suppliers, consultancy and 20 years with end-users. He is now an independent consultant.

finance require that their members sign that they have kept themselves up to date (for example with new legal requirements). The Engineering Council, which includes the BCS, makes it a requirement of its 38 member institutions to provide support for CPD. Institutions take account of relevant CPD when assessing membership applications and upgrades.

Support for CPD is provided by many institions through:

- log books to record CPD history, plans and achievements;
- log book pages available free from the Web;
- provision of certificates to those who have achieved a specific annual level of CPD;
- branch and specialist meetings;
- register of training courses;
- support from trained mentors.

The mentor facility is provided by some institutions for those who need assistance in planning their CPD (some employers may not be able to provide adequate guidance). The mentor provides confidential one-to-one mentoring to assist the member to identify skills required and suitable training plans, normally once-off to set up CPD plans and if required occasionally to review plans and achievements.

CPD and the company

The best companies provide career planning, mentoring and work experience records. These may be recorded in an appraisal file, owned by the employer, or within an employee's log book. Unless the employer follows a recognised professional development scheme, you would be well advised to keep your own private CPD log book, cross-referenced to the company's log book. Your own log book will ensure you have your own permanent comprehensive records which cover all your activities – private, at different work locations within your current employer, and also previous employers.

CPD and you

CPD is solely for your benefit: institutions and employers can only assist. Usually CPD is self-assessed – only you know if a period of work experience or training meets your needs. If you cheat or shortchange on CPD it is yourself who will suffer, and possibly find yourself out of work. For these reasons the institutions will record your CPD but not normally assess its value.

Get yourself a log book

Do you already have a log book? If not, obtain or create one now. Your log book is a collection of all matters concerning your lifelong CPD. It is a private book including details of your plans and aspirations, education and work experience. Extracts from your log book will be invaluable when preparing your general and specific

CVs, applying for permanent or contract work and assisting you to show you meet the training and experience requirements of professional Institutions.

What your log book should contain

A log book should, as a minimum, include the following sections and proforma sheets:
Personal Information and Long-term Planning
• Personal and academic information sheets
• Gap analyses sheets – providing details of current and required skills
• Development plans
Annual Records
• Current year development plan and log of CPD undertaken
Work Experience
• Work experience sheets for each job completed or period of work
Supporting Sheets
• Copies of certificates, attendance sheets and references

The BCS log book consists of the above and also includes *Guidance for Members*, a 20-page booklet.

The BCS log book is available to all members (including students and graduates) at a nominal cost. Well-organised people automatically retain their records systematically; however, the log book simplifies the task and helps to avoid omissions. You could create your own log book, in the same way that you could create your own diary – most people prefer to purchase one!

Your log book should start with your certificates from school and only end when you retire.

CPD and the BCS

The British Computer Society requires that all professional members follow the

BCS code of conduct, which includes (clause 18):

'Members shall seek to upgrade their professional knowledge and skill and shall maintain awareness of technological developments, procedures and standards that are relevant to their field, and shall encourage their subordinates to do likewise.'

The Society is a member of the Engineeering Council and provides all of the above CPD facilities. It provides an optional log book and annual record card to its members in support of the above. On request the BCS will provide a mentor service for those who need assistance in planning their CPD. The CPD log book is for the sole benefit of its members.

The BCS also provides a Professional Development Scheme, which is compatible with the BCS log book and provides accelerated progress towards BCS membership.

Next step

Contact the BCS to get yourself a log book (and if appropriate to obtain more details of the CPD scheme). E-mail: cpd@hq.bcs.org.uk; or Tel: 01793 417417. For more general information and sample log book sheets refer to the Web sites for BCS (http://www.bcs.org.uk) and those appropriate to your chosen career or employer.

Computing professionals and their professional bodies

Professional is a term used in many occupations with slightly different meanings in each, but in every case it implies an expertise in and dedication to one's chosen occupation and maintaining high standards in it. An amateur in sport is one who enjoys their sport as a pastime, and probably works quite hard at it. In contrast, a professional sportsman or woman has chosen to commit all their efforts to the sport, in order to make a living at it and achieve their best performance.

Computing is all-pervasive both in our working lives and in our leisure activities. Unprofessional activities on the part of people employed in computing can impact not only on safety-related situations, such as aeroplane control systems or the Channel Tunnel signalling, where injury or death can result from faulty systems, but also on systems in business, commerce and industry. Faulty or inefficient systems operation can lead to serious financial consequences and loss of competitive edge, and in smaller organisations even to going out of business. It is therefore in the interests of the public that systems are of high quality and reliability.

The professional bodies

How do clients and employers identify the computing professional? How can they be sure that the professional matches up to standards? One way is to employ members of the appropriate professional body. A practitioner who has become a professional member has convinced their peers in the profession that they have the competence

Aline Cumming

Aline Cumming is a consultant in IT and Education. She was previously Head of the Education Department at the BCS, responsible for administering accreditation, liaison with the Schools Committee and matters such as collating the BCS response to DfEE consultative papers. Before joining the BCS, she taught mathematics and computing at secondary school, having previously worked in data processing as a computer operator and programmer. Her first post on leaving university was as engineering assistant with British Rail.

to practise. They will have signed an undertaking that they will adhere to Codes of Practice and Conduct. Furthermore, the professional body will take steps to discipline and in extreme cases expel any member who is not meeting standards.

In the professions of medicine, the law and accountancy, membership of the professional bodies also grants licence to practise. The appropriate body first has rigorous membership criteria and second monitors continuous professional development, without which the professional cannot legally continue to gain their living in the profession. Other professions, such as teaching, are moving in this direction. Practitioners in computing have not yet reached an agreement on licensing but it is being discussed.

The forum for these discussions is drawn from the professional bodies, which for computing and information systems engineering in the UK are the British Computer Society (BCS), Institution of Electrical Engineers (IEE), Institution for the Management of Information Systems (IMIS) and Institution for Incorporated Engineers (IIE). In particular the BCS and IEE, together with the Government's Health and Safety Executive, are defining the necessary competencies for licensing work in safety-critical systems.

The members of these professional bodies will, to paraphrase the Royal Charter granted to the BCS, establish and monitor standards in the industry and education, on behalf of the general public. This includes the conduct and practice of the occupation, both of the individual and the company where he or she works and education, training and continuing professional development.

Benefits of membership

The first benefit is professional status and recognition. Whether you work in business, industry, in teaching, carry out research, in large or small organisations, professional membership carries weight and could earn you more money.

The second benefit is the many forms of support that membership can give you.

The BCS and IEE have a network of local branches and Special Interest Groups, such as the Internet SIG or Human Computer Interaction SIG. This allows members to mix with their peers and offer mutual support and exchange of information on topics of common interest. They can attend talks given by experts in technical or business fields, or at the leading edge of research, which can contribute to their professional development.

Most bodies offer their members tangible benefits such as discounts on books and technical journals, professional indemnity insurance, holidays and loans.

Thirdly, membership provides opportunities to influence government policy, as the professional bodies bring matters of concern to the attention of the authorities and in turn are consulted by them. The BCS has, for instance, contributed to work on legislation such as Data Protection and Intellectual Property Rights.

Members also contribute to the development of the industry, for example members of the BCS were responsible for the formation of the Independent Computer Contractors Group.

Membership

All the bodies offer several grades of membership. They range from student, for those at the start of their careers and studies, to full member for which education, training and professional development are assessed, and finally fellowship, which is achieved in the BCS by both seniority and having contributed to the advance of the discipline.

The BCS, IEE and IIE are Engineering Institutions, authorised by the Engineering Council to grant Chartered Engineer or Incorporated Engineer status to members who are suitably qualified.

The BCS and IMIS offer professional examinations for those employed in the industry wishing to gain educational qualifications to enhance their career and support an application for professional membership. The Engineering Council also offers an examination.

In conclusion

Because we are so dependent on computer systems we must have a force of capable professionals recognised as able to develop, maintain and update systems in a responsible way. If you decide to join them, you can contribute to your profession and advance your own career by taking part in your professional body's activities.

Information

More information about the professional bodies mentioned in this article can be obtained as follows:

The British Computer Society, Customer Services, 1 Sanford Street, Swindon, Wilts SN1 1HJ
Tel: 01793 417 417
Fax: 01793 480270
E-mail: bcshq@hq.bcs.org.uk
www.bcs.org.uk

Institution of Electrical Engineers
Michael Faraday House
6 Hills Way
Stevenage
Herts SG1 2AY
Tel: 0207 240 1871
Fax: 01438 313465
www.iee.org.uk

The Engineering Council, 10 Maltravers Street, London WC2R 3ER
Tel: 0207 240 7891
Fax: 0207 240 7517
E-mail: staff@engc.org.uk
www.engc.org.uk

Institute for the Management if Information Systems, 5 Kingfisher House, New Mill Road, Orpington Kent BR5 3QG
Tel: 0700 0023456
Fax: 0700 0023023
E-mail: central@imis.org.uk
www.imis.org.uk

Institution of Incorporated Engineers, Savoy Hill House, Savoy Hill, London WC2R 0BS
Tel: 020 7836 3357
Fax: 0207 497 9006
E-mail: info@iie.org.uk
www.iie.org.uk

finding the
right job

ding the right job finding the right job finding the right job finding the right job finding the right job finding the rig

Selecting an employer

It is difficult, if not impossible, to categorise all the different ways there are to work in the information systems industry. It is one of the most diverse and hybrid engineering disciplines and one that affects every single one of us in our everyday life, from the PC on our desks to the engine management systems in our cars and the complex safety-critical systems used, for example, in transportation and power generation systems. This complexity means that the industry can offer a massively wide range of job opportunities across a number of disciplines.

There are, however, some generalisations that can be made as to the sort of employment you could encounter. There are two main types of information systems employer, those who are systems developers or manufacturers and those who use the technology. There are also two types of each employer, large and small to medium enterprises (SME).

Large v. small

There is an important requirement for any prospective employee before they decide upon employment in any organisation, large or small. Careful research and questions at the interview will ensure that whatever company you choose it will be right for you.

The smaller company will give the IS employee a greater involvement in the organisation. It is likely that you will encounter a more varied remit than

Wilf Voss

Wilf Voss joined the British Computer Society in 1995 after graduating with a computing studies degree from South Bank University. He was responsible for student and graduate marketing as well as systems development in Microsoft Access and Office. He has now joined the European Computer Driving Licence team, and is involved in marketing and accrediting test centres.

those who work within the more structured world of the large organisation. You can become part of a closely formed team where there will normally be less formality relating to procedures and reporting structures. This can foster a great feeling of being a strong and integral part of the company, meaning that your efforts and contributions can be quickly rewarded.

However, you should consider the risks involved with smaller companies. A large company may lose a major customer and feel the effect, but a similar situation for a smaller company could put them out of business. Any dip in the profits will become apparent far more swiftly in the smaller organisation. The viability of any company should be part of your early investigations and you should continue to monitor this while you are employed. Look out for danger signs and be ready to move out if the situation arises.

> "Careful research and questions at the interview will ensure that whatever company you choose it will be right for you."

You should also be aware that, whereas many large companies will have structured training and development schemes allowing you to develop your skills, this may not be so simple in the smaller organisation. Nevertheless the SME might spend every penny wisely by ensuring you develop up-to-date skills to meet the needs of their business while the larger one may not use their training budgets so effectively.

Large companies will have a different way of working from smaller firms. They will have a more formal structure (a necessity because of their size and number of employees), with separate departments dealing with product development, support, marketing etc, and this can provide a great deal of flexibility so that the employee can find the right niche from which to forge a career. Employees will often be able to move between departments, changing the scope of their employment, and because of the more rigid organisational structure there can be a clearer career path through the chain of management.

Many large organisations in the IS sphere employ a team-based approach, meaning that as specific projects reach fruition the team is reorganised. This change of structure can give you experience of working with different people, different management styles, and on differing projects. This, and the fact that many large organisations will provide training and consider that employee development is an important factor, can help you build a strong professional career. Many organisations will provide work experience for new employees within different areas or departments to give an overall view of the organisation and its products, and support this with continuing development and training to allow them to keep their skills up to date in a fast-moving industry.

As membership of a relevant professional body becomes more important you should consider your future and whether your employment will match the requirements for professional membership. Both the BCS and IEE have accelerated membership routes for those who have been part of their accredited training courses (which are provided by many of the larger organisations in the industry).

The large company is also likely to provide a range of benefits that may not be provided by the smaller companies, including specific periods of leave, sick leave and pension schemes. Also there are the additional benefits of staff social facilities, sports facilities and subsidised catering.

Generally, there is no way you could say that working for a large company is better than working for a smaller company. You need to weigh up the pros and cons in your own mind; you need to decide whether you will prefer the close-knit environment offered by a small company or the more structured environment in a large company. It will be whatever suits you. There can be many challenges to be had working in a small company, taking a share of the credit and the profit when projects succeed, whereas larger organisations can offer you a wide range of experience across the organisational structure.

The developer v. the user

Now if you have made your decision about what scale of organisation you wish to work in, you need to consider the scope of their work. You may wish to be involved with development or with a user-based perspective.

You need to think what you would like to do as a career. Read through this careers guide and the reviews of each of the jobs, thinking not only for today but also for your future. You need to think seriously about where your skills lie. Are you an analytical person who enjoys the development involved with creating systems? Or would you prefer a more 'people'-oriented career, perhaps involved with user support or IS management, where you will be required to deal with a number of people on a daily basis? Of course you could become involved in a career that will involve you with both, dealing with user specifications, analysis and design.

For any career one of the most important attributes is interpersonal skills. It is essential to get on with people, whether they are working in a development team or are your users who have encountered a problem. It is as important to be able to express yourself and communicate your ideas as it is to listen.

Development companies will in general have a range of products and they will be responsible for the life-cycle of those products, not just the coding and programming, but the analysis and design, testing, implementation, maintenance and support. There are roles available across the range of activities and each can be very satisfying, from the analysis and design of systems to completing code or correcting bugs.

User-based companies are at the other side of this equation. They will use the developers' systems and IS staff will be responsible for the implementation, installation, use and support of those products. There are also the essential services required to keep a computer system running efficiently, as well as reviewing the security, maintenance etc. You are likely to be dealing with users on a daily basis, solving problems and looking for solutions. Generally there are many more user-based organisations than there are developers, and you could be involved in virtually any industry.

Getting a job

There is no simple way to find a job that will sidestep a lot of research, planning, administration and practice. Probably the most important thing to do, especially for your first job, is to start the process of looking as soon as possible. If you wait until the marketplace is flooded with graduates you will find that the best jobs have gone and most of the large employers' deadlines have passed!

Before you decide upon a career you should sit down and make a list of the things you enjoy doing in information systems and where your skills lie. Try to think seriously if you would be suited to development or more with the users of computer systems. Try to find out as much as you can about each job, and about individual employers.

You should then ensure that you have the groundwork ready for applying for jobs: write your CV (there are many guides available to help you with this), look in your careers centre, bookshop or library. For many employers, especially larger employers, you may be asked to fill out an application form. If this is the case please remember one thing: read the instructions and never commit ink to paper until you are totally ready! Make sure that you hand-write the form if that is what is required. Remember also that working out what you are going to write is best done on a piece of blank paper before you write on the form (mistakes and correcting fluid may not show you at your best!).

You should apply for as many jobs as will be suitable for you. Don't expect to apply for just one: you will need to apply for a number at a time and this will need real administration. You should keep a diary and ensure that if and when you are offered an interview you arrive at the right place at the right time.

Driving tests, exams and interviews are most people's worst fears, and an interview can be a nerve-racking experience. You should try to relax – remember that the employer is looking for someone like you. Listen carefully to the interviewer, smile and try to answer the questions calmly and clearly. Interview technique is something that can be improved with practice. See if your local careers service, mature friends or colleagues can help you with some practice interviews.

As part of a job application you may be asked to complete psychometric tests: these are structured ways of finding out how people perform on tasks or react to different situations. Most of the preparation for these tests is already complete; it is your current skills that are being tested, and practice is unlikely to improve your scores. The actual tests are restricted and are only released to those people who are trained in their use too; if they were generally available their effectiveness as selection tools would be lost. However, most careers service centres will have suitably trained staff and they may be prepared to run practice sessions with sample papers.

One of the most important aspects of getting a job is coping with a bit of rejection. Unfortunately, not everyone will get a job on their first attempt. If you are not selected you should just keep trying. If you have done your research and administration properly you should be successful eventually: just file away the details for the future, consider any work you have done as useful practice and reach for the next application form. When you succeed, remember to accept only one job offer. If you cannot make up your mind between two ask for more time to decide.

Above all, good luck!

key recruiters

AMP UK plc

Company

AMP is a leading international financial services group and in the UK operates six businesses: Cogent, Henderson Investors, London Life, NPI, Pearl and also has a 50% ownership of Virgin Direct. We control over £65 billion of assets worldwide on behalf of over 4.5 million customers.

Our range of products and services embraces life assurance, the provision of pension funds, investment management and administration, banking and general insurance.

Vacancies

Our training programme offers the right people first class training and experience. Role specific training and interpersonal skills development will be tailored to your needs and interests to help you gain specialised business expertise.

Entry requirements

Please check our website

Website

Visit www.AMPcareers.co.uk for further information about the programme.

Type of business: Financial Services

Number of employees: 19,000 worldwide

Number of graduate vacancies: Approx. 10 - check website

Starting salary in the region of: competitive

Other benefits: Numerous - check website

Areas recruited to: Trainee programmers

Main contact details: Kate Haller, USP Recruitment Co-ordinator, AMP UK plc, 3 Finsbury Avenue, London, EC2M 2PA

Other locations: Peterborough, Tunbridge Wells

How to apply: CV and covering letter quoting reference IIT2001

Closing date for applications: Refer to website

AMP

a unique proposition

Your handwriting* is one of the most distinctive things about you.

Because you have your own unique slant on the world, we think you'll appreciate a career package that's as individual as you are.

As one of the UK's best-known financial services groups, we are succeeding because we recognise the value of individuality and novel thinking. And whether you want to gain general or specialist business expertise, our Unique Solutions Programme aims to nurture your originality.

We want to find creative people who will breathe life into our industry, help us make a difference to the lives of our nine million customers, and fashion our business for the future.

If you're fascinated by invention, driven by curiosity and ambition, and think you can bring distinctive new approaches to our daily work, the Unique Solutions Programme could be for you.

Find out more by visiting our website **www.AMPcareers.co.uk**

Or send your CV with a covering letter, quoting reference ICA2001, to:
**Louise Barney, USP Recruitment Manager, AMP UK PLC,
3 Finsbury Avenue, London EC2M 2PA.**

* Please note that graphology is not used by AMP as a recruitment tool.
In fact, we're happy to accept online application forms.

gent   Henderson Investors   London Life   NPI Securing Your Financial Future   PEARL   Virgin direct 50% AMP owned

Andersen Consulting

Profile

Andersen Consulting is the world's leading management and technology consulting organisation. We specialise in working with our clients to improve their business performance by combining our in-depth industry skills with people, processes, technology and strategy. We utilise existing knowledge and apply it to new challenges in order to help our clients create their future. Our 1999 revenues were $8.9 billion.

Joining the team

In the emerging electronic economy sharing ideas can lead to new outlooks and new opportunities to succeed. By joining Andersen Consulting, you'll help transform world-class organisations as they compete for leadership in the future. Working with major corporations to implement large, complex projects is a team game so we are looking for team players who are outgoing and adaptable and have good communication skills. An interest in information technology is a necessity, although no previous experience in technology is required. Our way of working can also involve extensive travel so full mobility is essential.

If you're interested in working on challenging assignments within a dynamic culture that fosters knowledge-sharing, thrives on team-building and rewards great thinking, consider Andersen Consulting. We believe there is no more exciting place to be than where people are creating the future.

Our people make the difference

In the eCommerce world it is people who see the potential, adapt to suit the challenge and take action to make business ideas succeed. Andersen Consulting recognises people as the driving force behind our business and because of this, there is a dynamic environment that encourages our people to grow and learn within the company.

In addition to on-the-job learning, we provide a formal programme unmatched in the industry, spending US$595.5 million on training last year alone. The type and frequency of training offered to our professionals depends on previous experience, career level, client responsibilities and career track.

Training starts with an induction that focuses on developing IT and business skills while strengthening presentation and communication skills. After the initial training, there are on-going courses offered and everyone is encouraged to seize the opportunity to develop new skills.

Elective training starts at Consultant level and continues for all levels above. Each year, those at Consultant level and above are given a number of days to spend on elective training which they choose themselves from a wide range of classroom and self-study training courses.

Whilst formal training plays an important role in the development of skills and knowledge, it is only one component of our professional development. Within the firm, continual learning opportunities exist with the aid of tools such as the Andersen Consulting Knowledge Xchange, the firm's internal knowledge network where colleagues provide advice based on their own experiences. We also have 'communities' which provide a supportive base for everyone in the organisation to share information and get to know one another.

Show you've done your research. Please quote Inside Careers when responding to this profile.

... Andersen Consulting

A sophisticated career development framework ensures that everyone receives accurate and frequent performance feedback, sufficient on-the-job training, mentor support and career counselling.

People set the pace, both as a team and individually. Performance and drive will determine how far you go within the firm. Analysts can be promoted to Consultant level in as little as eighteen months and within five years new joiners can reach Manager level. Hard work and success pay off with promotions and opportunities within Andersen Consulting.

Type of business: Management and Technology Consultancy

Number of employees: 65,000 worldwide

Number of graduate vacancies: 300-400

Starting salary in the region of: A +£30,000 package

Other benefits: joining bonus of £1,750, paid overtime, private healthcare, contributory pension scheme, 20 days paid vacation each year

Disciplines recruited from: any degree discipline

Areas recruited to: Business and Technology Consultancy

Minimum degree class: 2.1 hons

Minimum UCAS points: 22 UCAS points or equivalent

Main contact details: The Graduate Recruitment Department, 2, Arundel Street, London WC2R 3LT

Online at www.ac.com/careers/uk

Tel - 0500 100 189

Other locations: Manchester, Newcastle, Dublin but full mobility is essential

How to apply: complete our online application form available on www.ac.com/careers/uk or call our free phone number 0500 100 189 for an application form to be posted to you

Closing date for applications: we recruit year round

AC Andersen Consulting

Arthur Andersen

Assurance, Risk Consulting - Technology

The ability to assess and manage a balanced perspective on IT related risk can give a business a significant competitive advantage. Working as an analyst in Technology you'll have the opportunity to develop your interest in IT whilst working across a range of industries. Your role will involve helping clients manage the risks of and maximise the benefits from eBusiness, run successful systems development projects and implement secure IT processing environments.

Tax Services - Technology Solutions

Technology Solutions provides innovative and individual solutions across a wide range of tax and technology issues internal and external to the firm. You could be working on online tax returns, accounts system integration projects from bespoke website design to employee adminstration systems and programming languages ranging from C++ to HTML.

Business Consulting

Arthur Andersen's Business Consulting arm is regarded by many within the industry as, "the new consulting kid on the block". The practice is split into four knowledge teams: Strategy, Finance and Economics, Advanced Technology, Business Process and People. Business Consulting works with the client to provide services including a broad range of e-commerce, process improvement, value-enhancement and technology-enabled solutions to improve decision making, business operations, organisational capability, and shareholder value.

Graduate Training

A variety of professional qualifications are on offer including the Certified Information Systems Auditor, the Microsoft Certified Professional, the Association of Tax Technicians and an MBA.

Type of business: One of the world's leading global professional services firm

Number of employees: Approx 74,000

Number of graduate vacancies: 650 vacancies

Starting salary in the region of: £25k - £28k (London)

Other benefits: Bonus scheme, interest free loan of up to £2,000, 21 days holiday, comprehensive training package

Disciplines recruited from: Any discipline

Areas recruited to: Assurance, Risk Consulting - Technology, Technology Solutions, Business Consulting

Minimum degree class: 2.1

Minimum UCAS points: 22

Main contact details: Director of Recruiting, Arthur Andersen, 1, Surrey Street, London WC2R 2PS. Email: lon-recruiting@arthur andersen.com. Website: www.arthurandersen.com/ukcareers

Other locations: Birmingham, Cambridge, Glasgow, Leeds, London, Manchester, Reading, St Albans

How to apply: Please refer to our website www.arthurandersen.com/ukcareers

Closing date for applications: None

ARTHUR ANDERSEN

Show you've done your research. Please quote Inside Careers when responding to this profile.

BLACK BOX

Who is Black Box?

Black Box is the leading source for networking connectivity. Based in Reading, Berkshire, with approximately 100 employees and a turnover in FY00 of £24 million, it is a wholly owned subsidiary of the Black Box Corporation in Pittsburgh, USA.

What do we do?

- The Black Box catalogue has over 10,500 products for all your networking solutions.
- On-site capabilities. Let us design, equip and install your network for you Anything from cabling infrastructure and UPS installations to office refurbishment's and electrical services.
- Free expert technical advice from 8am to 7pm, Monday to Friday.
- Dedicated account managers ensuring our customers get the best specialist for their needs.
- Custom capabilities. We can customise cables and products to suit customers.

What do we want?

We are looking for graduates with degrees in the IT area who want to join a dynamic and dedicated team within a global organisation. In Technical Support we are seeking enthusiastic and energetic engineers with good team-working skills and technical awareness who are looking to forge a career in the networking industry.

What do we give?

We offer a competitive salary package along with ongoing technical training.

To find out more visit us at www.BlackBox.co.uk

Type of business: Communications Solutions Provider

Number of employees: 96

Number of graduate vacancies: 5

Starting salary in the region of: £17,000 negotiable

Other benefits: Non-contributory pension, Health and Private Medical Insurance, Incentive and Productivity Bonus

Disciplines recruited from: IT, Electronic/Electrical

Areas recruited to: Network Solutions, Technical Support, Product Marketing, Product Support

Minimum degree class: 2.2

Minimum UCAS points: 16 or equivalent

Main contact details: HR Dept, Black Box (UK) Ltd, 464 Basingstoke Road, Reading, Berkshire, RG2 0BG Tel 0118 965 5000

Other locations: Vacancies based at Reading

How to apply: CV with covering letter quoting ref. IC to Elaine Graves (HR Department) at above address or email Elaine.Graves@ Blackbox.co.uk

Closing date for applications: Open

BLACK BOX
NETWORK SERVICES

Chase Manhattan Bank

An outstanding career.....

The Chase Graduate Development Programme holds the key to our success. Talented and enthusiastic graduates are essential to our continuing growth and the excellence of our training is recognised worldwide. There's no doubt, if you're thinking of a career in investment banking, then Chase should be top of your list.

What does a career at Chase mean to you?

- A truly international career
- Exceptional training and career development
- Excellent networking opportunities
- Lucrative financial rewards
- The flexibility to forge your own career path

Chase operates in over 45 countries, allowing us to offer you a wealth of international opportunities. Based in London, you'll be involved in the most challenging and stimulating projects in the industry and be excited by the fact that regularly you'll read about your work in the world's press.

We need to continue to attract the best of the best. You'll be part of a team and encouraged to share ideas and contribute to the development of strategies, products, services and systems. You'll certainly work long and hard, but remember - we also offer you a career with exceptional financial and personal rewards, including building a global network of business colleagues to last a lifetime.

Chase is one of the world's top-performing financial services firms. Let us tell you more about how you can join our growing success story. We can guarantee you a great experience, quality training and the chance to pursue an outstanding career.

Have you got what it takes?

Visit us at www.chase.com/graduates

Type of business: Investment Banking

Number of employees: Over 75,000

Number of graduate vacancies: 140

Starting salary in the region of: Competitive plus sign on bonus

Other benefits: Company pension, healthcare, gym

Disciplines recruited from: Any

Areas recruited to: Investment Banking, Global Markets (including Sales, Trading, Capital Markets, Research), Information Technology

Minimum degree class: 2:1 preferred

Minimum UCAS points: No minimum requirement but strong academic background preferred

Main contact details: www.chase.com/graduates

Other locations: London, Bournemouth

How to apply: Online

Closing date for applications: 15th December 2000

CHASE

THE RIGHT RELATIONSHIP IS EVERYTHING.®

IT Opportunities within Investment Banking

- Competitive Salary • City Based
- March 2001 and September 2001 Programmes

IT Graduates
Global Markets Technology

Are you interested in IT in the stimulating and challenging environment of Investment Banking? If so, one employer stands out from the rest: The Chase Manhattan Bank.

Our traders are some of the most successful in the world. Their achievements, however, stem not only from remarkable talents but sophisticated and innovative IT systems. Chase invests heavily in new technology and we will spend in excess of $2 billion on technology this year. More importantly though, we invest in our people. IT trainees join Chase's Graduate Training Programme, learning alongside the trading and sales trainees. Tailored IT content then prepares successful candidates for exposure to the trading IT departments through a series of challenging rotations.

We are currently looking for IT graduates to join our Global Markets Technology intake starting March 2001 and September 2001. Suitable candidates will be studying for an IT related degree or may have applied IT experience gained from extra curricular activities or work experience. A good academic background and an ability to demonstrate strong numerical skills is also required. To succeed you will need to be disciplined and accurate and work well within a team environment.

Our application form together with further information on Chase can be found on our website **www.chaseeugrad.co.uk** or by contacting our Graduate Recruitment Hotline on **0207 382 9848**.

CHP Consulting Ltd

Founded in 1990, CHP Consulting is one of the top twenty UK management consultancies to the financial markets. Our work primarily involves providing strategic and IT consultancy and software to blue chip companies such as Lloyds TSB, Abbey National, GE Capital, Halifax, IBM, Lombard, National Australia Group, Nissan, Société Générale and Siemens. Our expert knowledge of the finance industry and the partnerships we forge with clients before, during and after a project have enabled us to achieve a record of successful implementations which is unsurpassed.

As a growing, dynamic company, we provide the opportunity for each member of staff to make a real contribution to the development of the business and to take on responsibility as quickly as possible. Many of our current staff have left their previous employers (including Andersen Consulting, Logica and Hoskyns) to escape the 'small cog' feeling that can result from working for large employers.

Based primarily in the UK we have successfully completed consultancy projects throughout Europe in countries such as France, Germany and the Netherlands. We have also undertaken consultancy projects in countries throughout the world such as Australia. We are looking forward to continued growth world-wide.

Training

We provide regular training for all our staff. The standard training curriculum allows you the opportunity to develop business, technical, management and interpersonal skills. The training curriculum is constantly updated to reflect the changes in technology and the finance industry.

The training infrastructure covers information technology skills such as system design and development, functional skills such as finance and accounting, and consultancy skills such as writing reports and giving presentations.

Promotion is based entirely upon merit and we only recruit candidates who we believe have the potential to progress to the top of the company. The success of CHP is due to the quality of the people we employ. The considerable demand for our services, both from new clients and from existing clients, is proof of this and also of the high standard of software we provide.

Application Procedures

The Company is looking to expand functionally, technically and geographically in the coming year and opportunities exist for high calibre graduates to help us achieve this growth. Listed below are the key skills, knowledge and attributes we seek:

- University graduate with an Upper second or First Class Degree (preferably numerical)
- Excellent 'A' level results (Grades A and B)
- Outgoing, smartly presented, confident, articulate and a lateral thinker able to combine initiative and a logical approach with problem solving skills
- Excellent interpersonal and communication skills with the confidence to liase with senior client personnel.

In order to fit this profile you are probably currently in your final year studying a numerate degree at a top university. You may have some computing experience already, although this is not essential. You will have a

... CHP Consulting Ltd

proven academic track record to date and other achievements showing you to be motivated, successful and a self-starter.

The Rewards

Starting salary is £27,000 per annum plus £3,000 bonus upon commencing employment. Other benefits include private health insurance, life assurance, pension, generous holiday allowance and support for study required to gain further qualifications. A laptop computer is provided on joining.

Additional benefits such as profit related pay, company car and share options become available as you progress.

Apply by

CV with covering letter to Jo Gidman, Personnel Manager, Augustine House, 6A Austin Friars, London EC2N 2HA or email to jo.gidman@chp.co.uk

Company brochure available upon request.

To find out more about working with CHP Consulting Limited please refer to our CHP Careers page on our website at www.chp.co.uk

Type of business: IT Consultancy

Number of employees: 65

Number of graduate vacancies: 15

Starting salary in the region of: £27,000 plus a £3,000 bonus upon commencing employment

Other benefits: Private health care, life assurance, pension, disability insurance, profit related pay, generous holiday allowance

Disciplines recruited from: Any

Areas recruited to: Junior Consultant - working on a variety of client projects

Minimum degree class: 2.1

Main contact details: Jo Gidman, Personnel Manager, Augustine House, 6A Austin Friars, London EC2N 2HA; Tel: 0207 588 1800; Email: jo.gidman@chp.co.uk

How to apply: CV and covering letter or SAF

Closing date for applications: Ongoing

CHP Consulting

Data Connection Ltd

Data Connection is one of the world's most successful computer technology companies, working at the forefront of Internet communications technology. We develop high-quality, complex products for customers such as Cisco, IBM/Lotus, Microsoft, SGI and Sun. So, while you will not see our name in your local computer store, almost every new PC today includes some of our software - and we're working on products that you may well be using in 3 years' time.

We are developing our business to become world leaders in the explosive growth of voice and data network convergence. We are rapidly raising our profile within the marketplace and expanding our customer base. This means that there is more opportunity than ever for our employees quickly to take on significant responsibility.

Requirements

We are looking for exceptional people. Your superb academic background (successful applicants typically have all A's at 'A' level) must be complemented by good interpersonal skills, technical aptitude, energy and enthusiasm. We do not require any prior computing experience.

Career Development

Developing the skills and talents of our people is at the heart of what we do. We believe that the best way to learn is by doing real work in a well-disciplined and tightly managed environment. As a new graduate, your training will be specifically tailored to meet your individual needs and objectives, with constant support and expert guidance from your manager and mentor. This is enhanced by more formal internal and external education.

Type of business: Computer technology company

Number of employees: 200 as at June 2000

Number of graduate vacancies: 20-25

Starting salary in the region of: £25,000

Other benefits: Profit share, non-contributory pension, private healthcare and life assurance, social activities, morale events and company outings.

Disciplines recruited from: We recruit graduates and postgraduates from any discipline.

Areas recruited to: Product development, leading to opportunities in management, marketing and business generation.

Minimum degree class: N/A

Minimum UCAS points: Typically, successful applicants have all A grades at 'A' level.

Main contact details: Justine McLennan, Data Connection Ltd, 100 Church Street, Enfield, Middlesex EN2 6BQ.
Tel: 020 8366 1177; Fax: 020 8363 2927; Email: recruit@dataconnection.com

Other locations: Chester, Edinburgh, San Francisco and Washington, DC.

How to apply: Apply online at www.dataconnection.com or contact us at the above address for a brochure and application form.

Closing date for applications: None.

Show you've done your research. Please quote Inside Careers when responding to this profile.

The Defence Engineering & Science Group

The Defence Engineering & Science Group (DESG) is part of the Ministry of Defence civil service and is one of the largest employers of graduate engineers in the UK. The DESG is a group of civilan specialists responsible for ensuring that the UK has the most effective defence systems to defend the United Kingdom and overseas territories, our people and interests and to act as a force for good by strengthening international peace and security.

DESG is responsible for all aspects of MOD's equipment programme; from assessing requirements at the planning stage to disposal of equipment no longer required. We need people with an interest in defence who can grasp technical problems quickly, be innovative and manage change and staff successfully.

Your development

After successfully completing your training (normally two years) you drive your own development. You will typically spend two years in a job where you will directly apply your scientific and engineering expertise, followed by further jobs which develop your broader management competence. For those who maintain a rapid rate of development, the programmes offer early promotion to senior management within the DESG.

Type of business: Civil Service - Defence Engineering and Science Group

Number of employees: 17,000 engineers/sci

Number of graduate vacancies: approx 80

Starting salary in the region of: £16,014 - £17,423

Disciplines recruited from: Most engineering, computing and numerate degrees.

Areas recruited to: Defence equipment project management and throughlife support.

Minimum degree class: 2.2

Main contact details: Central MOD, Recruitment Office, PO Box 2443, Bath BA1 5XR

Other locations: through the UK and some overseas placements

How to apply: write to above address, tel: 01225 449106, www.desg.mod.gov.uk, e-mail: cmpers2b.mod@gtnet.gov.uk.

Please quote reference: IC (IT)

Defence Evaluation and Research Agency

The Company

At DERA, the Defence Evaluation and Research Agency, intelligence, imagination and innovation combine to produce next-generation research solutions for the MOD and an increasing number of commercial partners throughout the world. Ever ready to push back the boundaries of conventional thinking, our philosophy is to 'Think The Unthinkable'. Read on, and see what you think.

The Facts

Our stated aim is to be recognised as the world's foremost defence science and technology organisation. That's why we have developed a culture which encourages free thinking and promotes ground-breaking research. A culture which brings together the largest community of scientists and engineers in Europe and provides them with an ideal environment - plus unmatched facilities - for breakthrough achievement.

Unlimited scope. Exceptional scale.

A turnover in excess of £1billion...over 11,500 employees...research programmes spanning every dimension, from space and air to land and sea...this is the reality of DERA. From satellite communications to command and information systems, from structural materials to synthetic environments, the extraordinary range of our work offers unrivalled scope for people with a thirst for knowledge and an appetite for discovery.

Yet pioneering defence applications are only a part of our story. We're constantly exploring ways to harness the commercial potential of technology transfer. For example,

the crowded skies above us will become safer for travel thanks to our involvement in new-breed air traffic control systems. We invented flat-screen TV and ultra-thin loudspeakers (the latter via research into helicopter structures!). And our work in thermal imaging is now helping to save lives in earthquake survivor detection systems. This talent for originality, lateral thinking and knowledge sharing leads us into collaborations and joint ventures with commercial partners worldwide.

Who we attract

DERA is out of the ordinary, and so are the people who join us. We attract analytically-minded, innovative graduates from most IT, science, engineering and numerate disciplines.

Training & Development: a two-way commitment

Training programmes of the highest quality are designed to expand the talents of each individual and meet the needs of the business. We focus on building your commercial skills as well as your technical expertise. We provide you with a 'Resource Manager' to advise and guide you from day one. We encourage and support you to study for further academic qualifications such as an MSc or PhD or you can work towards achieving Chartered status. And we offer international opportunity through our involvement in collaborative partnerships and our presence at conferences worldwide. But equally, the onus is on you to take advantage of the training opportunities available and plot your own course of development.

... Defence Evaluation and Research Agency

We want your career at DERA to be rewarding, long-term and infinitely flexible. You could follow a technical path, becoming an accomplished specialist in your particular field, or move into technical management. Alternatively, you could take a business or project management route. Or you could pursue a career which interweaves the technical with the commercial. There is real scope for mind-broadening international assignments (we even offer foreign-language training). In short, it's all here.

A quality career. A great life.
High achievers deserve excellent rewards, which is why we offer starting salaries up to £20,000. High achievers also expect to be assessed on performance and promoted on merit - yet another attraction of DERA. And we're also firm believers in quality of life; all DERA locations lie in attractive areas away from urban sprawl, yet offer an appealing range of recreational, sports and leisure activities.

Further information
We have a mix of permanent and fixed-term appointments at many locations, dependent on your discipline and preferred area of work. The best way to discover DERA is to see us at first hand and meet us face-to-face, which is why DERA scientists and engineers will be attending recruitment fairs across the country, to answer your questions in person. Please contact us for a list of venues.

Type of business: Defence, Science and Technology Organisation

Number of employees: 11,500+

Number of graduate vacancies: 500+

Starting salary in the region of: Up to £20,000

Other benefits: DERA sites lie in attractive areas & offer a wide range of amenities. Generous pension & holidays

Disciplines recruited from: Most IT, Science, Engineering and Numerate disciplines

Areas recruited to: Operational Analysis, Scientific Research, Test & Evaluation, Project Management

Locations: Throughout the UK

How to apply: Graduate Recruitment, DERA Fraser, Eastney, Portsmouth, Hampshire PO4 9LJ
Tel: (023) 9233 5588
Email: Grad-Recruit@dera.gov.uk
Website: www.dera.gov.uk/careers

Closing date for applications: Ongoing

INVESTOR IN PEOPLE

DERA is a committed equal opportunities employer

DERA

Deutsche Bank

Who are we

Deutsche Bank has established its position among the global investment banking power-houses. Our worldwide network gives us a powerful platform allowing us to deliver superior results. We have built a truly global product range including debt and equity capital markets, advisory, fixed income and derivatives. Through BT Alex. Brown we greatly expanded our ability to serve global clients in all major markets and currencies and on all major exchanges of the world. We are also a pioneer in electronic business - our expertise shaping new opportunities for tomorrow's technology-driven markets.

Corporate Culture

Deutsche Bank is dedicated to being the best financial services provider in the world. We endeavour to make maximum use of our unique breadth of experience, capabilities and financial strength to create value for our customers, shareholders, employees and society as a whole.

Who are we looking for

We are looking for fresh innovative minds, creative spirits with a hunger to succeed. You will possess the natural drive that is a prerequisite to success in our business. You will strive to take ownership of your own projects with minimum supervision and you will reap the rewards we offer you as a result of your success. With carefully planned training and guidance you will safely and reliably deliver solutions and add value to our clients.

You need to be

- Inquisitive
- Analytical
- Numerate
- Logical
- Articulate
- Technical
- A team player

Type of business: Investment Bank

Number of employees: 92,000

Number of graduate vacancies: c.80 globally

Starting salary in the region of: £ competitive

Disciplines recruited from: Computer Science and related degrees

Areas recruited to: Global Technology and Services - into product aligned technology groups - for example OTC Derivatives, Foreign Exchange, Equities

Minimum degree class: 2.1

Minimum UCAS points: 22

Main contact details: www.db.com/careers

Other locations: London, New York, Frankfurt, Singapore, Tokyo, Sydney

How to apply: on-line application form

Closing date for applications: 01 December 2000

Deutsche Bank

It's the right time for global careers in information technology

Information Technology is the change agent, which is transforming the Investment Banking world.

At Deutsche Bank, IT forms the backbone for the business. You will work with some of the most advanced systems and the latest technology, developing and supporting mission-critical systems and applications for financial traders who demand high level performance to maintain a competitive edge in the market.

Working in an NT and UNIX environment, you will utilise tools such as Oracle, SQL, C++, VB, Java and the latest web technologies to assure the delivery of leading edge solutions that meet the needs of the bank now and in the future.

We offer an unrivalled training programme combining financial markets business knowledge with substantial IT technical training, which means you can make an immediate impact on the business

We are looking for ambitious, dynamic candidates to join our Global Technology and Services division within information technology. We want your global perspective, technical skills, outstanding communication abilities and commercial instinct.

If you are bright, articulate and enjoy a true challenge your time has come and you will thrive in this environment.

Performance in information technology – another reason why Deutsche Bank is leading to results.

www.db.com/careers

Performance is

leading to results®

Deutsche Bank

Dresdner Kleinwort Benson

Dresdner Kleinwort Benson is determined to be a significant player in the global investment banking market of the 21st century.

Our strategy hinges on a fully distributed global computer system that takes the power of IT directly to our customers - giving them the tools they need to make critical decisions on their risk management and control their costs. We have made a massive investment in leading edge technology to support this radical change management programme. We now need the exceptionally talented individuals who will drive its success.

At Dresdner Kleinwort Benson, you'll have an immediate opportunity to add value and make a difference on strategically important and high profile IT projects. Just when you thought your education was finishing, our approach to development will prove that it's barely started. Rewards are directly linked to performance and delivery. And with the organisation that means to become the dominant force in global investment banking, your career opportunities would be on a similar scale.

Type of business: Global Investment Bank

Number of employees: 3000 in London

Number of graduate vacancies: c50

Starting salary in the region of: £30,000 plus benefits

Other benefits: bonus, PPP, life assurance (x4 salary), pension scheme, free restaurant, season ticket loan

Disciplines recruited from: Any numerate. Exp JAVA, C++, PERL, Sybase, ActivateX, EJB, Corba, JSP a bonus

Areas recruited to: IT - you will join one of our infrastructure, development or support teams.

Minimum degree class: 2.2

Minimum UCAS points: 20

Main contact details: For futher information please see our website or email the address below

Other locations: Europe, N America, Latin America, Asia Pacific, Australasia and Africa

How to apply: Send your CV, quoting ref: IC to IT.recruitment@dresdnerkb.com

Closing date for applications: Recruitment ongoing

Dresdner Kleinwort Benson

Ernst & Young

Ernst & Young is one of the world's leading professional services firms. As information technology has developed, we have diversified our services to meet our clients' needs. They look to us to deliver technical solutions and ensure that the increasingly sophisticated information systems that underpin their global operations maximise their business performance. We are looking for graduates who want to develop their careers in this growth area of our business.

Information Systems Assurance & Advisory Services

We are a national practice providing a range of services to our clients which ensure that the business processes and information systems supporting their operations offer the degree of security and control they need, and any risks impacting their commercial success are minimised. Whilst you will already have an interest in the commercial applications of IT, our training will enhance both your technical and personal skills, allowing you to take responsibility from an early stage as a key member of project teams. The market for our services is growing rapidly as IT plays an increasingly central role in many businesses, and you can expect varied career opportunities as your knowledge and experience grows.

Minimum academics 22 UCAS points (excluding General Studies) and a 2:2 honours degree (any discipline).

Type of business: Professional Services

Number of employees: 6500 throughout the UK

Number of graduate vacancies: Vacancies in Bristol, Leeds, London, Manchester, Reading, Southampton

Starting salary in the region of: Competitive

Minimum degree class: 2:2 honours degree (any discipline)

Minimum UCAS points: 22 UCAS points (excluding General Studies)

Main contact details: Becket House, 1 Lambeth Palace Road, London SE1 7EU.

Website: www.ey.com/uk

How to apply: For a brochure and application form Freephone 0800 289208 or apply online www.ey.com/uk

Closing date for applications: Continuous recruitment process however you should apply early

ᴣ‖ ERNST & YOUNG

IBM (United Kingdom) Ltd

To lead the creation, development and manufacture of the world's most advanced information technologies is one thing. To spearhead an entire digital revolution is quite another. IBM is one of the largest IT companies, so of course we're at the cutting edge. We're established enough to boast 260,000 staff in 130 countries, but we're also fast-moving and flexible enough to be both the pioneers and principle exponents of e-business.

For example, we assisted Vauxhall to become the first UK car manufacturer to offer a range of cars exclusively over the Internet and we broke all records for the official Wimbledon Tennis Championships website. Demand for our hardware, software, services and expertise has never been greater. But it's the development of new ways for people to think, interact, manage their businesses and govern their lives that's the prime focus of our on-going innovation. Our size means we are big enough to tackle just about any area of new technology, but at the end of the day, it all comes down to the individual contribution of each and every one of our people.

Type of business: IBM United Kingdom is a global IT solutions provider and part of the world's largest IT company.

Number of employees: Approx.18,000 in the UK

Number of graduate vacancies: Approx. 400.

Starting salary in the region of: For our latest salary details see our website

Other benefits: Pension and Health Cover, bonus, 25 days vacation per year, sickness and accident cover, awards and recognition.

Disciplines recruited from: Any

Areas recruited to: Technical consultancy, systems specialists, software development, information systems, analyst programming.

Minimum degree class: 2.2 Honours degree

Minimum UCAS points: 18 UCAS points

Main contact details: www.ibm.com/employment/europe/graduate - see UK section. Email: 3grad@uk.ibm.com Telephone: 023 92 56 4015.

Other locations: IBM operates in over 25 locations in the UK including Basingstoke, Bedfont Lakes (near Heathrow), Edinburgh, Farnborough, Greenock, Hursley (near Winchester), Manchester, Portsmouth, Southbank (near Waterloo) and Warwick.

How to apply: We encourage you to apply online, throughout the year. Alternatively, you can request a brochure and CD rom by calling or emailing us at the details above or contacting your University Careers Service.

ING Barings

ING Barings is the corporate and investment banking arm of ING Group, employing over 9,300 people. We provide an extensive range of financial products and services to corporate and institutional clients around the world through a network of over 70 offices in 40 countries. We have a powerful presence in Europe, our home market, and a significant presence in the United States and Japan. In addition, we have a strong franchise in the emerging markets of Asia, Latin America and Eastern Europe.

Headquartered in Amsterdam and London, our global business is organised into three areas, Corporate and Institutional Finance, Equity Markets, and Financial Markets.

Corporate and Institutional Finance focuses on the origination and delivery of a full range of integrated solutions for corporations, financial institutions and governments. These include Mergers and Acquisitions and other advisory services, Debt Products, Equity Capital Markets, Lending and Private Equity.

Equity Markets offers institutional clients research, sales, trading and execution services across a wide range of equity based instruments (including futures and options on listed stocks, OTC derivatives and structured products) covering many different markets. ING Barings Equity Markets is active in the emerging markets of Asia, Eastern Europe and Latin America as well as the developed US, European and Japanese markets.

Financial Markets encompasses all our activities in asset and liability management, funding, international money markets, foreign exchange, fixed income and interest rate products and derivatives. Financial Markets offers sales and trading roles in both developed and emerging markets.

E-Business is a key area of the business that's developing fast. Working with the other business areas, it's a new venture to develop e-business solutions across ING Barings.

Training and Development

Having recently finished your studies, we will capitalise on the skills and experiences you already have and use them as a foundation on which to build a mutually beneficial relationship. During your induction programme, your development will follow a more formal structure and consist of classroom based training complemented by experiential learning. The specific nature of this training will be adapted to recognise the skill set you already possess and the specific requirements of the business that you will be joining. Enhancing your technical skills and product knowledge will be our top priority, although this will not be at the expense of developing your interpersonal and networking abilities. Throughout your career at ING, you will be encouraged to build a strong network with your colleagues around the globe.

Having completed the formal element of your induction training, you will progress into your business area, where you will undertake a training programme bespoke to that area. For certain business areas you will have the opportunity to undertake a number of rotations during your first 12 months that will help you determine your eventual role.

... ING Barings

Type of business: Corporate & Investment Bank

Number of employees: apprx 9300 worldwide

Number of graduate vacancies: 15

Disciplines recruited from: Primarily computing, technology, science & management related degrees

Areas recruited to: Technology planning, development, maintenance, management & strategy

Minimum degree class: 2.1

Minimum UCAS points: 24

Main contact details: Sarah Thompson, Graduate Recruitment. Tel: 020 7767 6944

Other locations: Europe, North America, Latin America, Asia

How to apply: Online Application only: www.ingbarings.com/careers

Closing date for applications: 24th November 2000

ING BARINGS

Innogy (the UK business of National Power plc)

The Company

Innogy, the UK business of National Power plc, is a major, integrated UK energy business comprising:

- a generation and trading business with a flexible, cost efficient portfolio of around 8,000 Megawatts of UK gas, coal and oil fired power stations, a leading energy trading capability and a competitive supply of fuels;
- npower, the national 2.6 million customer electricity and gas retail business which has been built from the combination of the MEB, Energy Direct and Calortex supply businesses;
- one of the UK's leading cogeneration and renewables businesses.

In addition the business has a power station operation, maintenance and engineering capability which is being marketed worldwide to secure third party external business, and innovative technologies are under development.

National Power plc has announced plans to demerge into two separate companies, an integrated UK energy business and an international power business. The demerger is due to be effective in October 2000.

IT Graduate Opportunities

We are seeking creative, customer-focused graduates who would positively welcome a fast changing culture. A good degree in IT or a related discipline is required combined with good commercial awareness and excellent communication and interpersonal skills.

A comprehensive training programme has been developed that focuses on your technical and personal development needs.

We've created the perfect framework to allow you to grow.

Innogy is committed to your continuous development and has achieved the 'Investors in People' standard throughout its business and we will invest in your future and ours by supporting and encouraging formal accreditation.

Type of business: Major Integrated Energy Business

Number of employees: approx. 4,000

Number of graduate vacancies: c.10

Starting salary in the region of: £17-18,500

Other benefits: Generous holiday entitlement, private health insurance, contributory pension scheme

Disciplines recruited from: IT and other disciplines

Areas recruited to: IT for all areas of the business-development, support & business analysis roles

Minimum degree class: 2.1

Minimum UCAS points: 18

Main contact details: Sue Beasley, ISD HR & Planning, Innogy, Windmill Hill Business Park, Whitehill Way, Swindon, Wiltshire SN5 6PB

Other locations: Swindon, Midlands

How to apply: CV and letter/Application Form/online

Closing date for applications: 30th March 2001

Innogy

KPMG

KPMG is one of the world's "Big 5" firms of business advisers, providing solutions to clients' business problems right across the globe. We have offices in 155 different countries staffed by nearly 100,000 people world wide.

If you choose to specialise in Information Risk Management (IRM) you will work with clients to ensure that they are using their information resources in the most efficient and secure way possible. Our IRM specialists deal in all aspects of IT risk, control, and security management and it is their job to focus on how technology can improve or transforms our clients' business process.

In the constantly moving arena of information and technology, it's a challenge to remain at the forefront of risk analysis, and to continue to offer appropriate design and implementation solutions. Our IRM specialists are drawn from a wide field of technological and business backgrounds and offer our clients outstanding IT expertise with a vital awareness of the wider business implications of the use of technology.

What type of people do we recruit?
If you like the idea of a career which combines an understanding of business with an appreciation of the importance of information and technology in today's world, then IRM might be for you.

We're looking for outstanding graduates, either straight from University or with some work experience, to join our national Information Risk Management team. A relevant degree and/or experience in the commercial use of IT is preferable but as a minimum you should have a keen interest in IT solutions and business issues, be capable of taking on responsibility at an early stage, and have good communication skills.

About the learning and development.
Our learning and development programmes are provided on a national and international basis, with courses covering both personal skills and specialist education in IRM services and issues. In London, there are two training options available. The first is the Chartered Accountancy (ACA) route and the second involves studying for an MSc in Information Security. In other offices, training is based around specific IT courses and on-the-job experience. Over two months of the first year is set aside to personal skills training. After three to four years there is also the opportunity to study for an MBA.

What some of our recent trainees think
"When a client said to me recently "I wish I had your job", I thought, yes, I'm glad I've got my job. About half of our work is supporting the assurance teams. We go in ahead of the project to check that the client's IT systems are secure. If anyone can get into the computer and change figures, then of course the audit isn't going to make much sense.

Working in IRM is really varied. For instance, I was involved recently in working for a record company who wanted their IT processes analysed. And currently I'm looking at a share settlement system for a financial client to ensure that it's secure from unauthorised access.

I'm not long back from a two-week project in Jamaica which wasn't as much fun as it sounds! It was a good example of how you have to adapt quickly to unfamiliar business

... KPMG

cultures. It was a challenge to assimilate boxes full of reports and information the day we landed so we were up to speed for a client meeting the following morning.

After a fortnight of working late and early starts I was ready to come home. But we got the job done and the client was well satisfied. I think that's why I'm glad I have my job. There's real job satisfaction." (Clare Patterson, London office)

Type of business: Business Advisory - Big 5

Number of employees: 10,520

Number of graduate vacancies: 650

Starting salary in the region of: £competitive

Other benefits: flexible benefits package

Disciplines recruited from: any discipline

Areas recruited to: IRM

Minimum degree class: 2.1

Minimum UCAS points: 20

Main contact details: telephone 0500 664 665 or visit www.kpmgcareers.co.uk

Other locations: 25 offices nationwide

How to apply: apply on-line via our website at www.kpmgcareers.co.uk Our on-line application process means that you will be guaranteed a response within 48 hours.

KPMG

logica

Think IT

Live IT

Enjoy IT

global IT careers

Logica has over 30 years' experience of delivering complex, mission-critical systems to key market sectors worldwide. We offer an all-embracing service, from strategic consultancy and innovative software products to systems integration, solutions delivery and outsourcing. We are known for being always a step ahead in how we think and the way we deliver. We need more high-quality graduates with the same flair and desire to find the technical solutions to help businesses perform better.

Logica

Introduction
Founded in the UK in 1969, Logica provide consultancy and information technology solutions to meet the business needs of leading organisations worldwide. Logica have around 8,500 staff in 24 countries around the world.

Company background
Annual turnover for 1999 was over £659 million.

Our work covers a wide range of market sectors: finance, defence, government, energy and utilities, space, telecommunications and transport.

In the UK, Logica has offices in Central London, Leatherhead/Cobham (Surrey), Brentwood (Essex), Cambridge, Bristol, West Midlands, Reading, Manchester, Edinburgh and Aberdeen.

Overseas we are represented in Europe, North and South America, Asia Pacific and the Middle East.

Training and Development
InSight Induction, which usually takes place during your first week, introduces you to the business, the way Logica works and our core values. This is followed by InBusiness: after two or three months you will spend three days investigating how and where Logica conducts its business and the processes and methods we use. InProjects is a day course, undertaken four to six months after you join, and will be spent looking at the way Logica runs projects for clients. InTeams: after nine to twelve months, you will have a three day session investigating teamwork at Logica.

Type of business: IT Solutions and Techinical Consultancy

Number of employees: Worldwide 8,500; 3500 in the UK

Number of graduate vacancies: 350+

Starting salary in the region of: £18-21K for 2000

Other benefits: Share option scheme; medical Insurance; relocation allowance

Disciplines recruited from: Computer Science or any related numerical or logical discipline.

Areas recruited to: Software applications programming and analysis leading to project management and technical consultancy

Minimum degree class: 2.2

Main contact details: www.Logica.com /ukgraduates; email: ukgraduates@Logica.com Tel: 020 74462333

Other locations: Reading, Brentwood, Surrey, Manchester, Bristol, West Midlands, Edinburgh, Aberdeen, Cambridge and Worldwide

How to apply: Logica application form

Closing date for applications: No closing date

Management Systems Modelling Ltd

About MSM

MSM is a software house offering first class software development to clients all over the UK. We combine excellent business understanding with excellent technical skills and a heavy emphasis on customer satisfaction. Our reputation is very good, reflected by the fact that over 50% of turnover is repeat business.

Why choose MSM?

We believe that we can only succeed if we make our clients' businesses succeed. Our most positive marketing is achieved by recommendation and "word of mouth". We can only secure satisfied clients and repeat business by consistently providing the Best Business Solution, and we can only achieve this by building an outstanding team to service clients - and every member of the team must enjoy coming to work!

Who do we need?

We only employ graduates with excellent Computer Science-related qualifications, but to join the team candidates must also have the ability to think quickly and demonstrate common sense under pressure. Individual technical skills are unimportant but all projects use combinations of Delphi, ASP, Java, SQL, Javascript and HTML, plus various databases.

More information is available at www.msysm.co.uk

Type of business: Software development

Number of employees: 10

Number of graduate vacancies: 10

Starting salary in the region of: £17-22,000

Other benefits: £4,000 training, pension, life assurance, long term disability benefit, profit sharing bonus scheme

Disciplines recruited from: Computer science or similar

Areas recruited to: Software development team

Main contact details: Thomas Coles, Managing Director, MSM, Discovery House, Steamer Quay Road, TOTNES, TQ9 5AL

How to apply: Email CV to recruit@ msysm.co.uk

Closing date for applications: none

MSM

MANAGEMENT SYSTEMS MODELLING

Show you've done your research. Please quote Inside Careers when responding to this profile.

155

Merrill Lynch Europe plc

Merrill Lynch is a leading global financial management and advisory company with a presence in 43 countries across six continents. We serve the needs of both individual and institutional clients with a diverse range of financial services. Merrill Lynch Europe, Middle East and Africa is one of the firm's largest and fastest growing regions.

Graduates are offered the opportunity to work in the dynamic environment of one of the world's leading financial institutions, where technology is considered critical to maintaining our global leadership status in the industry. As an ambitious graduate, progressing in your career, Merrill Lynch will expect you to gain new skills and keep up with the latest developments.

The start of the programme includes an intensive training period in New York with the introduction to core technologies used including professional, business, technology, project analysis and design training.

Merrill Lynch technology leads the effort to deliver electronic trading solutions globally in the inter-dealer and institutional client markets.

You may develop and deploy applications to enable configuration and execution of electronic trades imperative to the success of Merrill Lynch Europe. You will be involved on projects from conception through development to implementation. Problems will be solved using different types of financial instruments, programming languages, time-zones and databases simultaneously ensuring a diverse working environment with the opportunity to be an essential member of the team.

Type of business: Financial Services Industry

Number of employees: Worldwide approx 67,000, London: approx 6,500

Number of graduate vacancies: In Europe: Full time vacancies - 200

Starting salary in the region of: Competitive starting salary

Other benefits: Pension scheme, healthcare, company gym are all included in the graduate package. Business casual attire is also worn.

Disciplines recruited from: Applications are welcome from any degree discipline. A keen interest in the business is expected to be demonstrated.

Areas recruited to: Merrill Lynch recruits into a wide range of business areas including: Debt Markets, Equity Markets, Human Resources, International Private Client Group, Investment Banking, Investment Managers, Operations and Technology

Main contact details:

graduate_recruitment@ml.com

How to apply: Applications must be made via the online form at www.ml.com/careers

Closing date for applications: 1st December 2000

Merrill Lynch

Micromuse plc

Funded as a network solutions reseller, Micromuse has quickly moved to the centre of the communications revolution. Our Netcool suite solves the hardest software problems for the world's most successful telecommunications firms, Internet service providers and corporate enterprises.

Micromuse went public in February 1998 on the Nasdaq National Market (ticker symbol MUSE). Since then we've experienced hyper-growth. We now have sales offices around the world and relationships with more than 90 channel partners on six continents. Netcool is also sold by a host of telecom and Internet industry giants, including Cisco Systems and Lucent Technologies.

And that's just the beginning. Our opportunity in the marketplace is fuelled by the growth of the Internet, increasing competition between service providers and the convergence of voice and data networks. We have no direct competition today and are heavily to extend our unparalleled technology to make sure that things stay that way. Imagine the possibilities!

Netcool has become one of the software industry's premier success stories because it solves complex problems in a simple way. It is designed to monitor large-scale networks in real-time, allowing network operators to quickly identify and address problems before they lead to trouble.

Type of business: Micromuse develops and markets software for service level providers

Number of employees: 450 Global

Number of graduate vacancies: Varies

Starting salary in the region of: £18,000 + per annum

Other benefits: Bupa membership, options, ESPP, Life Assurance, Permanent Health Insurance

Disciplines recruited from: Computer Science, Computing, Discrete Mathematics, or related discipline

Areas recruited to: Software Development Engineers, Test Engineers

Minimum degree class: 2:1

Main contact details: Katie Barber, EMEA Human Resource Manager, Micromuse plc, Disraeli House, 90 Putney Bridge Road, London, SW18 1DA

Other locations: USA

How to apply: Fax: 020 8877 6271; E-Mail: katie@micromuse.com

Closing date for applications: No deadline

micro muse M

The Netcool Company

The Fast Show

How quickly do you expect your career to take off?

At Micromuse, you'll be part of one of the fastest growing IT companies in the UK - and according to Business Week, the 8th fastest in the world.

You'll also be with the company rated by the Sunday Times as the No.1 Share of the Year - important when you consider that a superior salary package also includes a generous share option scheme.

But what's at the heart of this phenomenal performance?

We produce Netcool®, the world's leading service level management software. And even more importantly, Netcool's core development happens right here in London. So there's no hanging around waiting to get involved with the important stuff.

What are you waiting for? Skip straight to our entry in the employer profiles.

micro muse **M**

The Netcool® Company

Amazon.com. Excite. British Airways. Yahoo. These are just a few of the companies, all leaders in their industries, that rely on Oracle to ensure the success of their e-businesses. With all ten of the world's largest websites relying on Oracle and eighty percent of the Web's most popular sites depending on Oracle's ability to handle huge numbers of users and enormous quantities of information Oracle is well positioned to play a giant role in the revolutionary decade to come. Indeed, Oracle's future is very, very bright: the kind of future that includes someone like you.

The challenge is continuous. With your 2:1 or above degree you will need to be instantly credible, confident in all situations, a quick thinker and have an ability to develop a sharp business sense. In return you can expect unrivalled training in Oracle and an excellent salary and benefits package including a company car.

To apply visit our web site at
http://jobs.oracle.com/graduates

Oracle Corporation (UK) Ltd

The Internet Changes everything...

Oracle is the world's leading supplier of software for information management, and the world's second largest independent software company. With annual revenues of more than $10.0 billion, the company offers its database, tools and application products, along with related consulting, education, and support services, in more than 145 countries around the world.

With its headquarters in Redwood Shores, California, Oracle is the first software company to develop and deploy 100 percent internet-enabled enterprise software across its entire product line: database, server, enterprise business applications, and application development and decision support tools.

Oracle is the only company capable of implementing complete global e-business solutions that extend from front office customer relationship management to back office operational applications to platform infrastructure.

Graduates required...

Our policy is to recruit graduates from the finest talent available and we look for a certain type of individual. This is not a place where you can hide in the background. You have to be ready to rise to any challenge, and be prepared to take the initiative when ever expected.

Starting salary package

A competitive starting salary with a 'Select' benefits program allowing you to tailor your package to your own needs.

Contact for Application form

Applications through our website at http://jobs.oracle.com/graduates.

Type of business: IT Company, selling software solutions and Databases

Number of employees: 4,500 UK, 33,000 globally

Number of graduate vacancies: 30-100

Starting salary in the region of: £19,500

Other benefits: Company car, private healthcare, pension & employee share purchase plan. Plus a self select benefits package

Disciplines recruited from: Consulting,any discipline others;technical or science orientated degree

Areas recruited to: IT Consulting, Product (designer/developer 2000 and applications) and interactive services

Minimum degree class: 2.1

Minimum UCAS points: 18

Main contact details: Sarah McKissick, Recruitment Resourcer, Oracle Parkway, Thames Valley Park, Reading, Berkshire RG6 1RA. Tel: 01189245572.

Other locations: Reading, Hemel Hempstead, Solihull, Manchester, City of London

How to apply: Application is through our web site only http://jobs.oracle.com/graduates

Closing date for applications: No closing date

ORACLE®
Enabling the Information Age

PA Consulting Group

Company Background

Established almost 60 years ago, and operating worldwide from over 30 offices in some 20 countries, PA draws on the knowledge and experience of about 3,000 employees, whose skills span the initial generation of ideas and insights all the way through to detailed implementation.

PA focuses on creating benefits for clients rather than merely proposing them, and this focus is supported by an outstanding implementation track record in every major industry and for governments around the world.

IT Opportunities Available

We are looking for talented graduates to work within our IT practices, developing expertise in technologies such as rapid application development in mission-critical systems, enterprise-wide computing, database design, multimedia, networking and emerging technologies. We are also seeking specialists with skills in management sciences such as modelling and operational research techniques.

Training and Development

Graduates attend an intensive three-week residential training programme held at the PA Management Centre in Kent. This is a global programme and you will be joined by PA graduates from around the world. The programme focuses on developing your business, consulting, interpersonal and technical skills. You will also learn 'out in the field', working with clients under the supervision of more experienced consultants. This is complemented by practical experience to satisfy both your personal aspirations and the needs of the business.

Where appropriate, you will also attend practice-specific training. For example, graduates joining our IT groups are given a further two-weeks' intensive training in the tools of the trade.

Type of business: PA is a leading management, systems, and technology consultancy

Number of employees: About 3,000

Number of graduate vacancies: 150 world-wide

Starting salary in the region of: Competitive

Other benefits: Performance-related and joining bonuses, share ownership, car benefit, healthcare, and pension

Disciplines recruited from: Our IT groups are seeking graduates with IT-related, technical, numerate or science-based degrees

Areas recruited to: Strategy; IT; Technology & Innovation; and our Industry groups

Minimum degree class: 2.1

Minimum UCAS points: 22

Main contact details: Jackie Tompkins, Graduate Recruitment Co-ordinator, PA Consulting Group, 123 Buckingham Palace Road, London SW1W 9SR

Other locations: UK, Continental Europe, Scandinavia, Asia Pacific, North America

How to apply: Please apply via our Web site at www.pa-consulting.com. You can also dial our hotline to request a brochure and application form (020 7312 4616).

Closing date for applications: All year round

PA Consulting Group

PricewaterhouseCoopers

Firm history
PricewaterhouseCoopers is the world's largest professional services organisation. We help our clients solve complex business problems and measurably enhance their ability to build value, manage risk and improve performance in an Internet-enabled world.

Ours is a diverse fusion of culture and experience and with your unique qualities and abilities, you could be an important part of this. Working with colleagues from different business areas, countries and cultures gives you invaluable experience of how a global business operates as well as the opportunity to travel and experience this first-hand.

Range of clients and services
Information technology is of crucial importance to PricewaterhouseCoopers, as it supports every aspect of our business. We know that our business success depends on our ability to be at the forefront of technology and we offer high calibre graduates aspiring to pursue a career within IT, three different, but highly challenging careers:

Global Risk Management Solutions (GRMS): working with clients, GRMS addresses the risks associated with on-going business operations, systems, technology and major change initiatives ensuring that these changes do not compromise business controls. GRMS views consulting on change and risk in terms of opportunity. We offer career opportunities within - Controls & Assurance Services - Enterprise and Resource Planning - and Data Management.

Global Tax Technology (GTT): working in partnership with our Tax & Legal

consultants, GTT delivers global systems that boost efficiency and information sharing ensuring that these systems operate in a flawless manner, enabling our consultants to deliver a first class service to our clients. Within Global Tax Technology there are opportunities to develop your career in programming, analysis and design, or systems assurance.

Global Technology Solutions (GTS): working within PricewaterhouseCoopers GTS provides IT services, solutions and the support necessary to enable us to continue to provide clients with a top quality service.

We offer on-going training and development opportunities including the chance to study for a variety of IT relevant qualifications.

Whichever area you join, you will be encouraged to take on early responsibility and be given tailored training and support, which will continue throughout your career with us.

Number of graduate trainees required
65

Graduate requirements
As a guide, 2.1 in any degree discipline, minimum 22 UCAS points and a strong interest in IT. A relevant IT/Engineering degree is needed for both Global Tax Technology & Global Technology Solutions.

Starting salary
Competitive plus flexible benefits

... PricewaterhouseCoopers

Contact for brochure and application form

Please call Freephone 0808 100 1500, or visit our website at www.pwcglobal.com/uk/graduate_careers/

Alternatively, apply on-line or send our completed form (obtainable from your careers service, our Freephone number above or via our website), stating your preferred office, to the address on the form.

Application deadline

Ongoing, but we encourage early applications, particularly for pre-graduate schemes. Deadlines for overseas students requiring work permits do apply and are on our website.

Graduate Recruitment Office

No.1 London Bridge, London SE1 9QL.
Tel: 0808 100 1500.

Other UK Offices

10 of our 38 offices recruit into IT.

Overseas offices

Over 850 offices in 150 countries.

Number of professional staff

Over 16,500 throughout the UK.

Type of business: Professional Services Organisation

Number of employees: 150,000 worldwide

Number of graduate vacancies: 65

Starting salary in the region of: Competitive

Other benefits: Flexible Benefits Scheme

Disciplines recruited from: GRMS - any, plus a strong interest in IT. GTT/GTS - relevant IT Engineering

Minimum degree class: 2.1

Minimum UCAS points: 22

Main contact details: Call Freephone 0808 100 1500 for a brochure and application form

Other locations: 38 offices across the UK

How to apply: On-line or send application (obtainable from careers service, our website or freephone number), stating your preferred office, to the address on the form

Closing date for applications: Accepted all year

PRICEWATERHOUSE(OOPERS ®

Quidnunc

We are a leading global 100% e-solutions provider, employing some of the keenest e-thinkers in the business. Our approach to building e-businesses takes clients from strategy through build to support-through the entire e-business lifecycle in fact. Our teams integrate strategy, technical and creative experts into a single focused unit.

Stable and secure we've been a growing and profitable business for the last 12 years. With a corporate culture that promotes knowledge sharing and rewards individual achievement, our staff turnover is less than 10%.

Quidnunc is growing fast... which means lots of new roles, and promotion on the basis of individual merit. From graduate entry, new recruits can move on to developer and then senior developer roles quickly, then our employees are deciding whether to follow a career in project management, or to specialise in a technical lead role.

Quidnunc e-solutions are founded upon Quidnunc people - on the unique outlook and skills they can bring to our business. The people we recruit, the ways we develop them and how we structure project teams are all critical success factors. This is why we recruit innovative, technically capable graduates, providing them with both intensive induction and on-going training in state of the art tools.

Type of business: 100% e-solutions provider

Number of employees: 300 employees worldwide

Number of graduate vacancies: 50

Starting salary in the region of: £20,500 + £1,000 bonus

Other benefits: Private Healthcare, Pension plan, Share options, book buying policy, sabbaticals, secondments to overseas offices.

Disciplines recruited from: Computer Science, Electrical/Electronic engineering

Areas recruited to: Software Development

Minimum degree class: 2.1

Minimum UCAS points: Science A-levels grade A&B

Main contact details: Graduates@quidnunc.com
Graduate Recruiter
The Shoe Factory
26-28 Paddenswick Rd
London W6 OUB

Other locations: New York, San Francisco, Austin (Texas) and Berlin

How to apply: By CV preferably by email

Closing date for applications: January, although we do consider applications throughout the year.

quidnunc®

Reuters

Reuters is on the move. Join us, and you'll team up with 17,000 people in over 150 countries. People who work in the frontline of the e-business revolution; who are motivated by working for a leading brand name; who relish challenge and variety; who have international opportunities. Graduate programmes cover Business & Media Management, Technology Management, Consulting, Journalism and Financial Management. Each offers exposure to the latest thinking on Internet technologies and their impact in a changing world.

We are the world's leading electronic news and information provider with over half a million 'professional' users in some 52,000 global locations. Now, we are pioneering a new breed of e-business entrepreneurialism that will open up a global market of 60 million private investors, who will use the web to enhance their investment decisions in every market, at any time and anywhere in the world.

We need graduates who make new ideas happen, use technology to drive change, and can anticipate the future - not reach for the predictable. We need self-starters with inquisitive and intellectual minds, analytical talent and the energy to challenge conventional wisdom. All degree disciplines are welcome, although technology-related degrees are preferred for our Technology & Consulting Programmes.

Type of business: The top provider of news to the world's media, trading markets and the Internet

Number of employees: 17,000

Number of graduate vacancies: 50

Starting salary in the region of: Top 10% of graduate recruiters

Disciplines recruited from: All IT/Engineering/Science related degrees

Areas recruited to: Technology Management and Technology Consulting

Minimum degree class: 2:1 preferred

Minimum UCAS points: 20 points

Main contact details:
E-mail: ukgraduate.recruitment@reuters.com
Or write to: The Graduate Recruitment Team, Reuters, 85 Fleet Street, London EC4P 4AJ.

Other locations: Global

How to apply: Apply on-line - see our website at: www.reuters.com/careers/graduate

Closing date for applications: First closing date: 30 Dec 2000, but confirm by visiting website.

REUTERS :D

real life

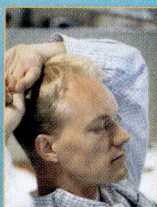

imagine no limits

Some people just want to earn a living. Others want to live their life.

They want to surround themselves with people bursting with energy, drive and commitment.

People who have access to technological resources that are second to none, in a business where IT makes the difference between success and failure.

They want to work in an open and honest environment where their ideas are listened to and where they're supported by the best training in the industry.

And they want to enjoy themselves while they're doing it.

This isn't a dream. It's real life. For all the facts and to apply for our graduate 2001 programme, go to our web site.

SCHRODER SALOMON SMITH BARNEY

A member of citigroup

Schroder Salomon Smith Barney

Company background

Schroder Salomon Smith Barney is a result of the merger between the investment banking business of Schroders Plc and Salomon Smith Barney. At the end of 1999, SSB was the second largest US based investment banking firm, as measured by profits and the third largest in terms of revenue. In terms of geographical balance, product range and sector coverage, Schroder Salomon Smith Barney is one of the world's foremost investment banks.

Joining us

When you join Schroder Salomon Smith Barney, you'll be joining one of the largest global finance and securities trading firms in the world. We were among the first to recognise that market opportunities are not limited by national borders. Today, we have significant operations in each of the world's major financial centres.

Information technology is at the heart of Schroder Salomon Smith Barney's business. It gives us the capacity to develop new financial transactions, manage risk, perform complex analyses of markets, keep the trading floor supplied with up-to-the-minute information and communications and ensure the swift and accurate execution of trades. We are as entrepreneurial in our use of technology as in every other aspect of our business. The constant challenge is to keep pace with rapidly changing business demands.

Graduates may work in business-aligned technology groups or alternatively may join one of the teams which provide specialist support. Roles in Global Technology are so varied, it would be difficult to describe a typical day in the department. You can experience almost any field of technology within our company - from networking, web development and programming, right through to support.

Initial training is followed by ongoing technical and business training. Our Mentor Programme and further appropriate courses also help to ensure continued professional and personal development.

Type of business: Investment banking

Number of employees: 3,500 throughout Europe

Number of graduate vacancies: 25

Starting salary in the region of: Highly competitive

Other benefits: Life assurance cover, Private Healthcare Plan, Pension, Interest Free Season Ticket Loan

Disciplines recruited from: All disciplines

Areas recruited to: Global Technology

Minimum degree class: 2.1

Minimum UCAS points: 24

Main contact details:
Web: www.careers-sssb.com

Other locations: Worldwide

How to apply: Online applications only.

Closing date for applications: 30th November 2000

SCHRODER SALOMON SMITH BARNEY
A member of citigroup

The Smith Group Ltd

The Smith Group provides the link between e-business strategy and the technology needed to deliver it. We offer a powerful combination of business and technology consulting - and the ability to follow through with the rapid development of innovative software where required.

We specialise in three areas:
- Customer Relationship Management;
- Mobile Internet;
- Information Security.

This focus, and a 220-strong team of people who combine imagination and technical ability with a practical, commercial approach, means that we offer industry-leading expertise. Speed of action in a fast changing world is what matters to our customers - and they value our agility, our innovative thinking and our objectivity.

We encourage people to take on responsibility, to think laterally and to focus on innovation - and thus help to solve our clients' wide-ranging business problems. We offer you the opportunity to make a radical difference to the business performance of our clients. You will see tangible recognition of your ability and the contribution you make; gain satisfaction from working on challenging tasks with like-minded people; and you'll be rewarded with structured appraisal and individual development schemes, plus a generous salary and excellent benefits package.

Type of business: e-business consultancy

Number of employees: 220

Number of graduate vacancies: 30

Starting salary in the region of: £22K-£25K

Other benefits: non -contributory pension, private health care, life assurance, relocation expenses and graduate loans

Disciplines recruited from: Numerate disciplines such as Computer Science, Engineering, Physics and Mathematics

Areas recruited to: consultancy and system implementation

Minimum degree class: 2.1

Minimum UCAS points: 28

Main contact details: Nikki Smith, Personnel Executive, The Smith Group Ltd, Surrey Research Park, Guildford GU2 7YP. Tel +44 (0)1483 442000. Fax +44 (0)1483 442203. Email: Recruit@smithgroup.co.uk. Website: www.smithgroup.co.uk

How to apply: CV plus covering letter to above address. Electronic applications are welcome

Closing date for applications: We recruit on an on-going basis

=Smith®

Standard Life Assurance Company

Standard Life is the largest mutual assurance company in Europe and one of the UK's leading financial institutions. Managing funds of over £70 billion, we combine immense financial strength with an outstanding reputation for service to our customers.

With one of the largest IT Divisions in Scotland, Standard Life presents a great opportunity for you to develop outstanding IT and business skills. As a trainee you will start your career in one of the following areas.

IS Development

Working in a development team could mean involvement in our strategic business projects focused on the timely provision of more flexible products to reflect the ever changing financial market place. Alternatively you may be involved in enhancing and maintaining our existing systems, helping to resolve today's business problems.

IS Operational Services

This area provides the IT services to meet daily business requirements. It also ensures the provision and enhancement of the infrastructure components enabling new functionality. These future requirements can be dictated by the demands of the financial sector or the opportunities available from emerging technologies, so the department must be both dynamic and receptive to change.

Training is tailored to the individual needs of each role. In addition there is on-the-job training and support for personal development. We offer a highly competitive package of salary and benefits. This includes a contractual bonus, non-contributory pension scheme, help with relocation costs, flexible working hours and private health care.

Type of business: Life, Pensions, Banking, Investments, Healthcare

Number of employees: 8,000 in Edinburgh, 11,000 worldwide

Number of graduate vacancies: 15-25

Starting salary in the region of: c. £18,700

Other benefits: contractual bonus, non-contributory pension, relocation assistance, private healthcare, house purchase scheme, flexible hours, sports and social clubs.

Disciplines recruited from: Applications considered from any discipline, although IT related preferred.

Areas recruited to: Development, technical support, customer service, e-commerce, analysis, technical architects, DBAs.

Minimum degree class: Any

Main contact details: The Graduate Team, Recruitment Department, Standard Life Assurance Company, Standard Life House, 30 Lothian Road, Edinburgh EH1 2DH. Tel: 0131 245 0587

Other locations: All IS trainee positions based in Edinburgh

How to apply: To apply please visit our website at www.individuals.co.uk

Closing date for applications: From October onwards

STANDARD LIFE

Show you've done your research. Please quote Inside Careers when responding to this profile.

Teleca Ltd

Introduction
Founded in Manchester in 1992, Teleca is a fast-growing software house providing development and consultancy services to blue-chip technology companies. We are part of Sigma AB (traded on the Stockholm stock exchange), a group of companies specialising in embedded software, e-commerce and engineering solutions.

Opportunities
We offer varied and challenging software development projects in leading-edge telecoms and internet technologies. Recent project areas have included: WAP, mobile phone applications, EPOC, smart card, workflow, digital TV, and GPRS.

Company Culture
Teleca has a friendly informal culture with casual dress, paid overtime, flexible hours, and excellent social activities. Most of our work is done in the UK, but some Teleca staff have recently worked in Scandinavia, Western Europe and Japan. Career progression is limited only by ability - our growth provides plenty of opportunities!

Requirements
We are looking for bright enthusiastic graduates with good honour's degrees (at least 2:2) who have the ability to learn new technologies quickly, a positive attitude, and the flexibility to cope with a demanding industry. In addition, we require programming experience commercially or at university in C, C++ or Java.

Type of business: Software engineering

Number of employees: ~180 (Dec 2000)

Number of graduate vacancies: approx. 30

Starting salary in the region of: 17-20,000 + benefits

Other benefits: pension scheme, paid overtime, flexi-time, life insurance, loyalty scheme

Disciplines recruited from: computer science or any with experience in computer programming

Areas recruited to: software developers

Minimum degree class: 2.2

Main contact details: Recruitment, 634 Wilmslow Road, Didsbury, Manchester M203QX. Email: recruitment@teleca.com. Web: www.teleca.com

Other locations: Manchester, Winchester, Swindon

How to apply: CV and cover letter

Closing date for applications: ongoing

UBS Warburg

We have centres of excellence in all the world's key financial markets, established and emerging. Through 13,000 staff in more than 40 countries, we deliver global investment banking expertise to corporate, institutional and sovereign clients. Our approach has given us a leading position in Europe, in the Americas, and in the Asia/Pacific region - but we want more.

The key to achieving growth and change is recruiting the right people into the right culture and giving them every opportunity to achieve. Our commitment to personal and professional development ensures you have all the support you need. You will have the freedom to demonstrate your sophistication and strength of character in an environment where achievement and reward are naturally connected.

Information Technology and E-commerce are key drivers of UBS Warburg's competitive advantage in the global marketplace. The IT team develops and maintains the underlying technology platform and processing systems, covering the entire product range of investment banking products.

We're in the business of innovation and things move very quickly. It's a dynamic, challenging environment where IT and business staff work closely together to make sure that the business is benefiting from the latest technologies.

At UBS Warburg, IT means more than writing software. It's a holistic approach to ensure total service delivery. We are consultants, communicators, innovators, analysts and coordinators. We don't just see the business need and identify the best solution. If a pre-packaged system solution doesn't exist, we build one!

Type of business: A broad based Investment Bank

Number of employees: 13,000 globally

Number of graduate vacancies: 30 in IT dept

Starting salary in the region of: £35k + £3k sign-on

Other benefits: Full benefits including value-flex, medical insurance, pension plan etc..

Disciplines recruited from: Computer Science, Management Information, Engineering, Science, Maths.

Areas recruited to: Applications support/ , developing tactical IT solutions/systems development.

Minimum degree class: 2.1

Main contact details: www.ubswarburg.com

Other locations: London, Conneticut, Chicago, Tokyo, Singapore, Hong Kong, Sydney, Zurich

How to apply: Please apply via website using our on-line application system located on the careers section or our website www.ubswarburg

Closing date for applications: 1st Dec 2000

UBS Warburg

unlimited

JOIN ONE OF THE FASTEST GROWING INVESTMENT BANKS WHERE 20% OF OUR REVENUES ARE INVESTED INTO TECHNOLOGY

Ours is a fast-evolving, high stakes business where constant innovation is vital to maintaining our position as a top tier global investment bank. We have long recognised that Information Technology is the lever to that innovation.

If you want to work at the frontier of applied and emerging technology, you can do it with us. As a graduate, you will be exposed to the banks' diverse business, advanced processing concepts and proprietary application systems. As well as essential project and people management skills, you will acquire valuable development, implementation and e-commerce experience.

To apply for a graduate or summer internship position, please do so using our on-line application system at **www.ubswarburg.com**

UBS Warburg

Global careers in investment banking

UNISYS

Introduction

We are Unisys-a $7.5Bn company of 36,000 people dedicated to helping the world's leading banks, airlines, communications companies and public agencies get the most from technology. World-class employers don't come much better than Unisys. After all we've been around long enough to know what's what. But what makes us different is our outstanding employees who believe in their work and their organisation.

To ensure our graduates are fully prepared for the exciting challenges ahead, you'll join a team developing solutions or implementing new systems. As your experience increases your career may develop through a project management, business development, technical or solutions route.

Training

When you arrive at Unisys, you will begin an intensive training programme. This training programme covers essential business and interpersonal skills designed to orientate you in the company. After this initial baseline training our in-house University will provide you with a tailored made training path. This training is tied to your role and designed to equip you with the skills for success and career advancement.

Career developement

At Unisys there is no such thing as a dead-end career. Working together with your manager and mentors, you can develop the career you want. We've built the infrastructure to help you. For example we've mapped a career path for every role at Unisys, and we've built leading edge web tools to help you manage your career and keep it in tip-top shape.

Type of business: Information Services and Technology

Number of employees: 36,000 Globally

Number of graduate vacancies: 300 in the UK

Starting salary in the region of: from £20,000

Other benefits: Healthcare Plan, Pension Scheme, Life Assurance, 22 days holiday, Long-term disability, Stock purchase plan

Disciplines recruited from: Computer Science/IT or related degrees. Also opportunities for graduates with Business or related degrees.

Areas recruited to: Information Systems and Technology Consultants, Software and Hardware Engineers, Network Consultants, Programmers and Systems Analysts

Minimum degree class: 2.1preferred, although a 2.2 is acceptable

Minimum UCAS points: 16 UCAS points

Main contact details: Graduate Recruitment Team, Bakers Court, Bakers Road, Uxbridge UB8 1RG. Website: www.unisysukgrads.com Freephone: Gail Upton on 0800 917 9130

Other locations: 16 Location in the UK. Majority of vacancies in our Uxbridge, Slough, London, Glasgow and Milton Keynes offices.

How to apply: Application forms and brochures are available from your Career Service. Alternatively apply on-line at www.unisysukgrads.com or freephone Gail Upton on 0800 917 9130.

Closing date for applications: Continuous recruitment

UNISYS

Yellow Pages

Introduction

The famous Yellow Pages directory is probably our best-known product, but we are not just a classified paper directory business. Our portfolio also includes Yell.com, Business Pages, Talking Pages and the Business Database. From our solid roots in the UK, we took a giant stride into the US, acquiring Yellow Book USA in August 1999, and now Yellow Pages has 600,000 customers worldwide. As the way people access information has changed so have our products. We are putting more and more emphasis on our new media products, including our web site Yell.com which offers businesses and consumers a simple, fresh and exciting way to search for products and services on line. Through harnessing new technologies and developing new products and services we will continue our success into the future.

IT at Yellow Pages

The world of IT is changing fast and Yellow Pages is changing with it, so joining us as an IT graduate trainee will give you exposure to many exciting opportunities. There are a wide range of projects that you may be involved in, including e-commerce - internal, external and mobile, data factory, Internet, system software support and use of ERP - SAP to support core systems. This makes the Yellow Pages Graduate Programme the perfect training ground for ambitious young professionals, and through an intensive yet flexible 18-month development scheme, you will find your way to the area of the business that suits you best.

Type of business: An international directories and e-commerce business.

Number of employees: 5000 in both UK & US

Number of graduate vacancies: 2 - 3 in IT dept

Starting salary in the region of: £17,000 - £19,500

Other benefits: Financial assistance in relocation, bonus and contributory pension scheme

Disciplines recruited from: IT degree desirable, though not essential. Team player a necessity

Areas recruited to: All IT areas, including New Media

Minimum degree class: 2.2

Main contact details: Graduate Recruitment, Yellow Pages, Queens Walk, Reading RG1 7PT. Email: jobs@yellowpages.co.uk - please mention graduate in title

How to apply: Please send your CV and covering letter explaining why you would be suitable to the address above.

Closing date for applications: 16 February 2001

YELLOW PAGES®
www.yell.com

STUDENTS & GRADUATES

What can the British Computer Society do for you?

Save you money and keep you up-to-date with Industry issues

- Reduced rates on membership
- Discounts on a wide range of services
- Free subscriptions or special offers on industry magazines and books
- Free access to information services
- Free lifetime e-mail address

Maximise your potential

- Finding the right job
- Networking
- Professional Membership
- Continuing Professional Development

www.bcs.org.uk/joinbcs.htm

Tel: 01793 417417
Fax: 01793 480270
Email: marketing@hq.bcs.org.uk

BCS

quick reference table

This table provides summary information on employers of graduates into IT. If a company has detailed information in the *Key recruiters* section then a page number is provided in the left-hand column.

Page	Company	Type of business	Employees	Vacancies	Starting salary (£)	Benefits	Disciplines recruited from
	3com Europe Ltd	multidisciplinary IT company	13,500 world	20–25	20,000	share purchase schemes, profit share, private health, pension, life assurance, relocation allowance	computer science, electrical, mechanical, software and production engineering
	Abbey National	retail banking	19,000	100	18,000–20,000	company pension scheme, bonus	all
	ABN AMRO	investment banking	2,000+ UK	c. 50		flexible benefits scheme, performance-related bonus	all – however, business-related degrees more relevant
	ALSTOM Power Conversion Ltd	engineering	c. 1000	c. 20			
	Altran	consultancy	8,000	200		medical insurance, life assurance	computer science, software engineering, engineering-related
	American Management Systems (AMS)	large consultancy	9,000+ world			employee stock purchase plan, health insurance, pension plan, flexible working hours	all, interest in IT is essential, one European language preferred
128	AMP UK plc	financial services	19,000 world	c. 10		numerous – check website	
130	Andersen Consulting	management and technology consultancy	65,000 world	300–400	30,000	joining bonus of £1,750, paid overtime, private healthcare, contributory pension scheme	any
	ARM Ltd	intellectual property: RISC processors	518	100	21,000–23,000	stock options; SAYE; profit sharing (12% for past 2 yrs); life/pension/medical	electronic eng; computer science; software eng
132	Arthur Andersen	professional services	c. 74,000	650	25k–28k London	bonus scheme, interest-free loan of up to £2,000, 21 days' holiday, comprehensive training package	any
	Artsoft Ltd	IT software and solutions	22		20k	bonuses	Oracle

The companies that have a tick in the BCS column are accredited participants in the British Computer Society's professional development scheme.

Areas recruited to	Degree	UCAS points	How to apply	Closing date for applications	Contact	Other locations	BCS
eng, hardware/software, applications tools, manufacturing, test production			online	31/01/01	Graduate Recruitment, Boundary Way, Hemel Hempstead, Hertfordshire HP2 7YU. Tel: 01442 438 000	Eire, Edinburgh	
graduate trainee scheme	2.2	14	online	none	Sam Endell, Recruitment Services, Abbey National plc, PO Box 964, Abbey House, Milton Keynes MK9 1AG. Web: www.abbeynational.plc.co.uk/recruitment		✓
wholesale banking, private clients and asset management	2.1	24	online	01/12/00	Lisa Pickup, Graduate Recruitment Manager, 250 Bishopsgate, London EC2M 4AA. E-mail: Lisa.Pickup@uk.abnamro.com Tel: 020 7678 7005; Web: www.graduate-uk.abnamro.com	over 74 countries worldwide	
electrical, electronic, software			CV, EAF, SAF	31/03/01	Graduate Recruitment, Personnel Department, ALSTOM Power Conversion Ltd, Boughton Road, Rugby CV21 1BU. E-mail: personnel.rugbr@powerconv.alstom.com	customer sites worldwide	
IT, telecommunications, defence, aeronautics, space electronics, banking			CV	ongoing	Richard Letzelter, Newspaper House, 8–16 Great New Street, London EC4A 3NP	UK and across Europe	
			CV and letter	ongoing	Ms Nidhi Gaur, Bezuidenhoutseweg 12, The Hague 2594 AV, Netherlands. Tel: +31 70 3787197;E-mail: Nidhi_Gaur@ams.com; Web: www.ams.com	across Europe	
trainee programmers			CV and letter quote ref. IIT2001	Refer to website	Kate Haller, USP Recruitment Coordinator, AMP UK plc, 3 Finsbury Avenue, London EC2M 2PA	Peterborough, Tunbridge Wells	
business and technology consultancy	2.1	22	online or freephone	all year	The Graduate Recruitment Department, 2 Arundel Street, London WC2R 3LT. Web: www.ac.com/careers/uk; Tel: 0500 100 189	Manchester, Newcastle, Dublin	
design engineers; software engineers	2.1	24		none	Graduate Recruiting Dept., ARM, 110 Fulbourn Road, Cambridge CB1 9NJ. E-mail: hr@arm.com, Web: www.arm.com	Cambridge, Sheffield, Maidenhead, Paris, Nice, Munich, Korea, Japan, USA	
assurance, risk consulting – technology, technology solutions, business consulting	2.1	22	online	none	Director of Recruiting, Arthur Andersen, 1 Surrey Street, London WC2R 2PS. E-mail: lon-recruiting@arthurandersen.com; Web: www.arthurandersen.com/ukcareers	Birmingham, Cambridge, Glasgow, Leeds, London, Manchester, Reading, St Albans	
software engineers	2.1	18	online	n/a	Pip Gould, HR Executive, 106 High Street, Ripley, Surrey, GU23 6AN. Web: www.artsoft.co.uk	Ripley/Surrey	

Page	Company	Type of business	Employees	Vacancies	Starting salary (£)	Benefits	Disciplines recruited from
	AT&T	communications, networking, information services	4,000 in EMEA	c. 20	20,000	8% bonus, pension, private medical insurance, life assurance, 25 days' holiday etc	IT, communications, other 'logical' disciplines
	Avesta Sheffield Ltd	manufacturer of stainless steel	6,000+ world	10	16,500	flexible working, occupational health facilities, lump sum bonus (after 12 months), pension scheme	computer science, information systems, information technology
	BAE SYSTEMS	aerospace and defence systems	100,000+	500	17,500– 20,500	£2,000 joining bonus, pension, healthcare, share option and car scheme	engineering – all related disciplines, business
	Barco Ltd	industrial automation technology	4,500 world	c. 2	18,000– 20,000	profit bonus, merit bonus, pension scheme, life assurance, 24 days' holiday, PC purchase scheme	computer science, electronic engineering, maths
133	Black Box	communications solutions provider	96	5	17,000 neg.	non-contributory pension, health and private medical insurance, incentive and productivity bonus	IT, electronic/electrical
	The Boots Company plc	health and beauty products	80,000 world	80		relocation allowance; 25 days holiday; staff discounts; contributory pension scheme	any
	Cambridge Technology Partners (UK) Ltd	business and technology consultancy	200 UK and Ireland	25+		pension, bonus, private healthcare, subsidised gym membership, 2-week training in US, 23 days' vacation	computer science
134	Chase Manhattan Bank	investment banking	75,000+	140		company pension, healthcare, gym	any
136	CHP Consulting Ltd	IT consultancy	65	15	27,000 + 3k bonus	private healthcare, life assurance, pension, disability insurance, profit-related pay, generous holiday allowance	any
	Citrix Systems (Research and Development) Ltd	application server software and services	200 UK, 1,200 world		21,000	stock options; pension scheme; BUPA; permanent health insurance; life assurance; holidays – 23 days	computer science or IT-related
	Computacenter	distributed systems and services supplier	4,500	30	18,000	bonuses, non-contributory pension, PHI, share-save	any
	Consort Securities Systems Ltd	software development	130	5	16,000	pension scheme, private medical ins, life assurance, profit bonus	any

Show you've done your research. Please quote Inside Careers when responding to companies.

Areas recruited to	Degree	UCAS points	How to apply	Closing date for applications	Contact	Other locations	BCS
operations, service mgt., network design, integration and deployment, finance	2.2		CV	all year	Julie Fowler, AT&T Human Resources, Highfield House, Headless Cross, Redditch B97 5EQ	Redditch, Portsmouth, London, Warwick	
graduate training scheme	2.1	22	EAF	31/12/00	Graduate Recruitment, Avesta Sheffield Ltd, PO Box 161, Shepcote Lane S9 1TR. Tel: 0114 2443311	Panteg, South Wales, Oldbury, West Midlands	✓
software, systems, electronic and mechanical engineering and business functions	2.2	18	EAF, online	31/07/01	BAE SYSTEMS, Graduate Resourcing, 32 Aybrook Street, London, W1M 3JL. E-mail: baegraduaterecruitment@tmpw.co.uk, Web: www.baesystems.com/graduate	over 60 sites in the UK	
software development, systems engineering	2.1		CV	all year	Mrs Eryl Leach, Barco Ltd, Dextralog Division, Whitebirk Estate, Blackburn, Lancs. BB1 5SN. E-mail: eryl.leach@barco.com; Web: www.barco.com	Belgium	
network solutions, technical support, product marketing, product support	2.2	16	CV + letter quote ref. IC, e-mail	open	Elaine Graves, HR Dept, Black Box (UK) Ltd, 464 Basingstoke Road, Reading, Berkshire, RG2 0BG Tel: 0118 965 5000 E-mail: Elaine.Graves@Blackbox.co.uk	vacancies based at Reading	
graduate development programme			online	30/06/01	Graduate Recruitment Manager, The Boots Company plc, D31 Nottingham NG90 4HQ. E-mail: Graduate.recruitment@boots-plc.com; Web: www.bootscareers.com	Nottingham; West Midlands	
graduate developers in IT	2.1		CV and letter	31/12/00	Claire Sims, 72 Lower Mortlake Road, Richmond, Surrey, TW9 2JY. Tel: 020 8334 6800; E-mail: UK-Recruiting@ctp.com; Web: www.ctp.com	Richmond, Reading, Dublin, Manchester, plus 49 other offices worldwide	
investment banking, global markets (including sales, trading, capital markets, research), information technology	2:1		online	15/12/00	Web: www.chase.com/ graduates	London, Bournemouth	
junior consultant – working on a variety of client projects	2.1		CV and letter, SAF	ongoing	Jo Gidman, Personnel Manager, Augustine House, 6A Austin Friars, London EC2N 2HA. Tel: 020 7588 1800; E-mail: jo.gidman@chp.co.uk		
software development, software test, software localisation, technical support	2.1		CV by e-mail		Recruitment Team, E-mail: recruitment-high-wycombe@eu.citrix.com; Tel: 01494 493148;Fax: 01494 684996	High Wycombe, Cambridge, Dublin, Germany, France, The Netherlands, USA	
IT, sales, project management, business analysis	2.2	12	online	all year	Tel: 01707 639990 (queries); Web: www.computacenter.com	most positions are in Hatfield, Herts but we do recruit across UK	
help desk, software support, analyst programmer, systems analyst, tester	2.2	16	CV and letter	ongoing	Mrs Kerry Mackinder, Personnel Manager	none	

Page	Company	Type of business	Employees	Vacancies	Starting salary (£)	Benefits	Disciplines recruited from
	CS Rand	software solutions and services	110	10	16–20k	comprehensive flexible benefits, pension, PHI, life, medical, dental, critical illness	computing or related disciplines
138	Data Connection Ltd	computer technology company	200	20–25	25,000	profit share, non-contributory pension, private healthcare and life assurance, social activities, morale events	any
139	The Defence Engineering and Science Group	civil service	17,000 eng/sci	c. 80	16,014–17,423		most engineering, computing and numerate
140	Defence Evaluation and Research Agency	defence, science and technology	11,500+	500+	up to 20,000	DERA sites lie in attractive areas and offer a wide range of amenities. generous pension and holidays	most IT, science, engineering and numerate
	Delcam plc	developers of CAD/CAM software	230	4	16,000	free medical insurance, contributory final salary pension scheme	engineering, computer science, mathematics, physics
	Deloitte & Touche	professional services firm	8,000	20			IT-biased, ideally with business focus
142	Deutsche Bank	investment bank	92,000	c. 80			computer science and related
144	Dresdner Kleinwort Benson	global investment bank	3,000 London	c. 50	30,000	bonus, PPP, life assurance (x4 salary), pension scheme, free restaurant, season ticket loan	any numerate. exp Java, C++, Perl, Sybase, Activatex, EJB, CORBA, JSP a bonus
	EDS	IT services	13,000+ UK	300+		health and dental scheme, life insurance	maths, physics, computer science – any plus a practical interest in IT
	Efunds International	software solution provider	130 UK, 3,000 USA	3		pension, private health, long-term sick cover, bonus, 25 days' hols, subsidised gym membership	computer related, pref. computer science
145	Ernst & Young	professional services	6,500 UK				
	Ford Motor Company	design and produce vehicles	30,000 UK	c. 100	21,500+	benefits include car purchase scheme, 26 days' annual vacation, co. pension and sports facilities	any

Areas recruited to	Degree	UCAS points	How to apply	Closing date for applications	Contact	Other locations	BCS
junior programmers	2.2		CV and letter	variable	Martin Jeffery, Human Resources, Northbrook House, Oxford Science Park, Sandford on Thames, Oxon, OX4 4GA. E-mail: martin_jeffery@rand.co.uk	Edinburgh	
product development, leading to opportunities in management, marketing and business generation		30	EAF, online	none	Justine McLennan, Data Connection Ltd, 100 Church St, Enfield, Middx EN2 6BQ. Tel: 020 8366 1177; E-mail: recruit@dataconnection.com; Web: www.dataconnection.com	Chester, Edinburgh, San Francisco and Washington, DC	
defence equipment project management and through-life support	2.2		letter, quote ref: IC (IT)		Central MOD, Recruitment Office, PO Box 2443, Bath BA1 5XR. Tel: 01225 449106; Web: www.desg.mod.gov.uk; E-mail: cmpers2b.mod@gtnet.gov.uk	through the UK and some overseas placements	
operational analysis, scientific research, test and evaluation, project management				Ongoing	Graduate Recruitment, DERA Fraser, Eastney, Portsmouth, Hampshire PO4 9LJ. Tel: 023 9233 5588; E-mail: Grad-Recruit@dera.gov.uk; Web: www.dera.gov.uk/careers	throughout the UK	✓
software development, application engineering	2.1	20	CV or e-mail	none	Development Administrator, Delcam plc, Small Heath Business Park, Birmingham B10 0HJ. E-mail: jobs@delcam.com		
trainee consultants in management solutions and enterprise risk services	2.2	20	EAF, online, freephone	all year	Sarah de Cartere, Deloitte & Touche, Hill House, 1 Little New Street, London EC4A 3TR. Freephone 0800 323333; Web: graduates.deloitte.co.uk	London with national remit	
global technology and services – into product-aligned technology groups – for example otc derivatives, foreign exchange, equities	2.1	22	online	01/12/00	Web: www.db.com/careers	London, New York, Frankfurt, Singapore, Tokyo, Sydney	
IT – you will join one of our infrastructure, development or support teams	2.2	20	CV by e-mail, quote ref: IC	ongoing	E-mail: IT.recruitment@dresdnerkb.com	Europe, N America, Latin America, Asia Pacific, Australasia and Africa	
IT graduate training scheme	2.2	18	EAF, online	none	Nicole Brennan, 4 Roundwood Avenue, Stockley Park, Uxbridge UB11 1BQ. E-mail: ukgraduaterecruitment@eds.com; Web: www.eds.co.uk	UK wide from Aberdeen to Worthing	
software development	2.2		CV	30/04/01	Karen Gerrard, Personnel Administrator, eFunds International, Wingate House, Northway, Runcorn, Cheshire, WA7 2SX		
	2:2	22	online, freephone	ongoing, apply early	Becket House, 1 Lambeth Palace Road, London SE1 7EU. Freephone 0800 289208; Web: www.ey.com/uk		
IT, HR, purchasing, marketing and sales, engineering, finance and Ford credit			online		Web: www.ford.co.uk/recruitment	Essex, Merseyside, Southampton, South Wales, Leamington Spa and Daventry	✓

Page	Company	Type of business	Employees	Vacancies	Starting salary (£)	Benefits	Disciplines recruited from
	Government Communications Headquarters (GCHQ)	government intelligence and security agency	4,500	c. 100	16,000	non-contributory pension scheme, flexible working hours, full- and part-time positions, sports and social	IT, computing, electronics, communications, maths, physics, information science
	Hewlett Packard	information technology	120,000 world	c. 50	From 20,000	pension, private healthcare, life assurance, 25 days' holiday, cash profit sharing, share scheme	IT, computer science, electrical and electronic engineering and business
	HSBC	banking	40,000 world	215	17,000–20,700	£2,000 joining bonus and banking benefits	any
146	IBM (United Kingdom) Ltd	global IT solutions provider	c. 18,000 UK	c. 400	see website	pension and health cover, bonus, 25 days' vacation per year, sickness and accident cover	any
147	ING Barings	corporate and investment bank	c. 9,300 world	15			primarily computing, technology, science and management-related degrees
149	Innogy (the UK business of National Power plc)	integrated energy business	c. 4,000	c. 10	17,000–18,500	generous holiday entitlement, private health insurance, contributory pension scheme	IT and other disciplines
	Keane Ltd	multidisciplinary IT company	500	40	18,500	flexibility allowance, company pension, PRP	IT, computer science, physics
151	KPMG	business advisory – big 5	10,520	650		flexible benefits package	any discipline
153	Logica	IT solutions consultancy	3,500 UK, 8,500 world	350+	18–21k	share option scheme; medical insurance; relocation allowance	computer science or any related numerical or logical discipline
	Lucent Technologies	telecomms	150,000 world	c. 70	19,000+	25 days' holiday, sick pay, pension scheme, healthcare, 6 monthly pay reviews on the graduate scheme	computer science, electrical/electronic eng, physics, maths, business-related
155	Management Systems Modelling Ltd	software development	10	10	17,000–22,000	£4,000 training, pension, life assurance, long-term disability benefit, profit-sharing bonus scheme	computer science or similar
	Mars	information services– global IT business of Mars		5–10	24,000	private healthcare, life assurance, generous pension package	combined IT/business or other related degree and a strong interest in IT required

Show you've done your research. Please quote Inside Careers when responding to companies.

Areas recruited to	Degree	UCAS points	How to apply	Closing date for applications	Contact	Other locations	BCS
technologists, IT specialists, communications and electronics engineers	2.2		EAF	varies	Recruitment Office, Room A1108, GCHQ, Priors Road, Cheltenham GL52 5AJ. Web: www.gchq.gov.uk; Tel: 01242 232 912/3; Fax: 01242 260 108		
IT, consultancy, sales, marketing and finance	2.1	18	online	end Dec	Web: www.jobs.hp.com	Thames Valley, London, Manchester and Birmingham	
large number of IT trainee positions	22	12	online	ongoing	Viv Andersen, IT HR, GHIII, 41 Silver Street Head, Sheffield S1 3GG Tel: 0800 289 529. Web: www.banking.hsbc.co.uk	Sheffield and some areas in London	
technical consultancy, systems specialists, software development, information systems, analyst programming	2.2	18	online		E-mail: 3grad@uk.ibm.com; Tel: 023 92 56 4015; Web: www.ibm.com/employment/europe/graduate	over 25 locations in the UK	
technology planning, development, maintenance, management and strategy	2.1	24	online	24/11/00	Sarah Thompson, Graduate Recruitment Tel: 020 7767 6944; Web: www.ingbarings.com/careers	Europe, North America, Latin America, Asia	
IT for all areas of the business-development, support and business analysis roles	2.1	18	CV, letter, EAF, online	30/03/01	Sue Beasley, ISD HR and Planning, Innogy, Windmill Hill Business Park, Whitehill Way, Swindon, Wiltshire SN5 6PB	Swindon, Midlands	✓
analyst programmer, solutions developer	2.2		CV	all year	Graduate Recruitment Keane Ltd, Oscott Rd, Witton, Birmingham B6 7UH Tel: 0121 332 3476; Web: www.keane.uk.com; E-mail: grad_recruitment@keane.uk.com	nationwide	
IRM	2.1	20	online		Tel: 0500 664 665; Web: www.kpmgcareers.co.uk	25 offices nationwide	
software applications programming and analysis leading to project management and technical consultancy	2.2		EAF	none	E-mail: ukgraduates@Logica.com; Tel: 020 74462333; Web: www.Logica.com/ukgraduates	Reading, Brentwood, Surrey, Manchester, Bristol, West Midlands, Edinburgh, Aberdeen, Cambridge and worldwide	
software, hardware, systems, test, technical support, some commercial vacancies	2.1	18	online		Graduate Recruitment Office, Lucent Technologies, The Quadrant, Westlea, SN5 7DJ. Web: www.lucent.co.uk	Swindon, Malmesbury, Chippenham, Ascot	
software development team			CV by e-mail	none	Thomas Coles, Managing Director, MSM, Discovery House, Steamer Quay Road, Totnes, TQ9 5AL. E-mail: recruit@msysm.co.uk		✓
IT development programme			EAF, online	24/12/00	Mars Graduate Marketing, Dundee Road, Slough, SL1 4JX. Tel: 01753 514999; Web: www.mars.com/university	Wokingham, 23 European sites	

Page	Company	Type of business	Employees	Vacancies	Starting salary (£)	Benefits	Disciplines recruited from
156	Merrill Lynch Europe plc	financial services industry	c. 6,500 London, c. 67,000 world	200 Europe		pension scheme, healthcare, company gym are included; business casual attire is also worn	any
158	Micromuse plc	develops and markets software for service level providers	450 world		18,000+	BUPA membership, options, espp, life assurance, permanent health insurance	computer science, computing, discrete mathematics, or related discipline
	National Grid	electricity transmission	3,500		18,100	BUPA healthcare, pension, sports facilities on larger locations, discounts at high street chains	any IT- or computer-based degree
	Nestlé UK Ltd	food and drink manufacturer	10,000	c. 30	c 20,000	relocation assistance, performance-related pay	all degree disciplines accepted
	Nortel Networks	telecommunications	90,000 world	350	19,500 min.	flexible benefits scheme	comp. science, engineering, maths, physics and other technical related
160	Oracle Corporation (UK) Ltd	IT company, selling software solutions and databases	4,500 UK, 33,000 world	30–100	19,500	company car, private healthcare, pension and employee share purchase plan, plus a self-select benefits package	consulting, any discipline others; technical or science orientated degree
	Oxygen Solutions Ltd	systems integration and consultancy	80	c. 10	22,000	flexible benefits scheme, including pension, private healthcare, gym dental plan	computer science or any with experience in computer programming
162	PA Consulting Group	management, systems, and technology consultancy	c. 3,000	150 world		performance-related and joining bonuses, share ownership, car benefit, healthcare, and pension	IT-related, technical, numerate or science-based
	PA News Ltd	media, news and sports results service	1,000			pension, life insurance, interest-free season ticket loan	IT-related
	Praxis Critical Systems	software and systems consultancy	c. 100	6	20,000	25 days' holiday, life insurance, BUPA, personal accident, long-term disability, sports and social	scientific and numerate
163	Pricewaterhouse Coopers	professional services organisation	150,000 world	65		flexible benefits scheme	GRMS – any, plus a strong interest in IT. GTT/GTS – relevant IT engineering

Areas recruited to	Degree	UCAS points	How to apply	Closing date for applications	Contact	Other locations	BCS
areas include: debt markets, equity markets, human resources, international private client group, investment banking, investment managers, operations and technology			online	01/12/00	E-mail: graduate_recruitment@ml.com; Web: www.ml.com/careers		
software development engineers, test engineers	2:1			none	Katie Barber, EMEA Human Resource Manager, Micromuse plc, Disraeli House, 90 Putney Bridge Road, London, SW18 1DA	USA	
information services group (ISG) based in Brookmead (Guildford)	2.2	18	letter, e-mail, online		Graduate Recruitment, National Grid Company, National Grid House, Kirby Corner Road, Coventry, CV4 8JY. Tel: 024 76 537777; Web: www.nationalgrid.com	Coventry, Leatherhead, Wokingham, Leeds, plus other locations nationwide	
graduate development programme – information systems	2.1		EAF	22/11/00	Graduate Development Programme Manager, Nestlé UK Ltd, St George's House, Croydon, Surrey, CR9 1NR. Tel: 020 8667 5469; E-mail: nestlegrad@uk.nestle.com	throughout the UK	
diverse mix of technical and non-technical job families	2.2	18	online	ongoing	Web: www.nortelnetworks.com	various across UK and continental Europe	
IT consulting, product (designer/developer 2000 and applications) and interactive services	2.1	18	online	none	Sarah McKissick, Recruitment Resourcer, Oracle Parkway, Thames Valley Park, Reading, Berkshire RG6 1RA. Tel: 01189245572; Web: jobs.oracle.com/graduates	Reading, Hemel Hempstead, Solihull, Manchester, City of London	
professional services, support, consultancy	2.1		CV, letter	01/05/01	Professional Development, Oxygen Solutions Ltd, Regal House, 70 London Road, Twickenham, Middlesex TW1 3QS Tel: 020 8744 4600. E-mail: personnel@oxygen-solutions.com	Twickenham, Middlesex and Europe	
strategy, IT, technology and innovation, and our industry groups	2.1	22	online, hotline 020 7312 4616	all year	Jackie Tompkins, Graduate Recruitment Co-ordinator, PA Consulting Group, 123 Buckingham Palace Road, London SW1W 9SR. Web: www.pa-consulting.com	UK, continental Europe, Scandinavia, Asia Pacific, North America	
software development/support, technical support, customer services, editorial	2.2		CV	none	Jill Shiel, Editorial Manager, PA News Ltd, PA News Centre, 292 Vauxhall Bridge Rd, London SW1V 1AE. Web: www.pressassociation.com	London, Leeds, Howden	
software and safety engineering	2.1	22	CV, EAF	none	Helen FitzGerald, Praxis Critical Systems Ltd, 20 Manvers Street, Bath BA1 1PX. Tel: 01225 466991; E-mail: hlf@praxis-cs.co.uk	parent company with offices throughout Europe	✓
	2.1	22	EAF, online	all year	Freephone: 0808 100 1500	38 offices across the UK	

Page	Company	Type of business	Employees	Vacancies	Starting salary (£)	Benefits	Disciplines recruited from
165	Quidnunc	100% e-solutions provider	300 world	50	20,500 + 1,000 bonus	private healthcare, pension plan, share options, book buying policy, sabbaticals, secondments to overseas	computer science, electrical/electronic engineering
166	Reuters	news provider	17,000	50	Top 10%		all IT/engineering/ science related
	Schlumberger	oilfield service, IT, manufacturing	64,000	30			software, hardware and electronic eng, networking, programming C++, Java,
167	Schroder Salomon Smith Barney	investment banking	3,500 in Europe	25		life assurance cover, private healthcare plan, pension, interest-free season ticket loan	all
	SEMA Group	multidisciplinary IT company	6,300	200	16,000–22,000	25 days' leave, choice of insurances, pension	computer science but all others considered by exceptional candidates
	Siemens	electronic and electrical engineering and telecoms	16,000 UK	c. 100	min 17,500		any
169	The Smith Group Ltd	e-business consultancy	220	30	22–25k	non-contributory pension, private healthcare, life assurance, relocation expenses and graduate loans	numerate such as computer science, engineering, physics and mathematics
	Standard Chartered Bank	international bank	27,000 world	200 world		annual bonus, international share scheme, retirement benefit, concessional housing plan	any degree – with a strong interest in the financial markets
170	Standard Life Assurance Company	life, pensions, banking, investments, healthcare	8,000 Edinburgh, 11,000 world	15–25	c. 18,700	contractual bonus, non-contributory pension, relocation assistance, private healthcare, house purchase scheme, flexible hours	any considered, although IT-related preferred
	Strategic Thought	IT solution provider (consultancy and software house)	40–50			profit share, 10% of salary into group personal pension scheme, 23 days' holiday etc.	any, but a proven aptitude for computing an advantage
171	Teleca Ltd	software engineering	180	c. 30	17,000–20,000	pension scheme, paid overtime, flexi-time, life insurance, loyalty scheme	computer science or any with experience in computer programming
	TenFold Systems UK Ltd	IT	50	20	23,000	pension scheme, annual bonus, medical + dental insurance	any considered by exceptional candidates

Show you've done your research. Please quote Inside Careers when responding to companies.

Areas recruited to	Degree	UCAS points	How to apply	Closing date for applications	Contact	Other locations	BCS
software development	2.1	A& B in Sci	CV by e-mail	Jan, all year	Graduate Recruiter, The Shoe Factory, 26–28 Paddenswick Road, London W6 OUB. E-mail: Graduates@quidnunc.com	New York, San Francisco, Austin (Texas) and Berlin	
technology management and technology consulting	2:1	20	online	30/12/00	The Graduate Recruitment Team, Reuters, 85 Fleet Street, London EC4P 4AJ. E-mail: ukgraduate.recruitment@reuters.com	global	
hardware engineers, technical consultants, technical sales positions	2.1		online		Web: www.slb.com	Europe	
global technology	2.1	24	online	30/11/00	Web: www.careers-sssb.com	worldwide	
all			CV, EAF, online		John Lincoln, Graduate Recruitment Manager, 2 Killick Street, London N1 9AZ. Tel: 0207 830 4444; E-mail: recruitment@sema.co.uk; Web: www.semagroup.com	various locations across the country, including Scotland	
all			online, EAF	all year	Stacey Jackson, Siemens plc, Sir William Siemens House, Princess Road, Manchester M20 2UR. E-mail: Siemens@dial.pipex.com; Web: www.siemens.co.uk	all across UK	✓
consultancy and system implementation	2.1	28	CV, letter	ongoing	Nikki Smith, Personnel Executive, The Smith Group Ltd, Surrey Research Park, Guildford GU2 7YP. Tel: 01483 442000; E-mail: Recruit@smithgroup.co.uk; Web: www.smithgroup.co.uk		
	2.1		online	1/12/00	Sue Hayes, Standard Chartered Bank, 1 Aldermanbury Square, London EC2V 7SB. E-mail: Sue.Hayes@uk.standardchartered.com; Web: www.standardchartered.com	UK, several countries in Asia and Africa	
development, technical support, customer service, e-commerce, analysis, technical architects, DBAS	any		online	Oct onwards	The Graduate Team, Recruitment Department, Standard Life Assurance Company, Standard Life House, 30 Lothian Road, Edinburgh EH1 2DH. Tel: 0131 245 0587; Web: www.individuals.co.uk	all IS trainee positions based in Edinburgh	
IT development (e-commerce), network support, IT consultant	2.1		CV + letter by e-mail or post	varies	Strategic Thought, The Old Town Hall, 4 Queens Road, London SW19 8YA. E-mail: ecruit@strategicthought.co.uk	project work opportunities around the UK and abroad	✓
software developers	2.2		CV + letter	ongoing	Recruitment, 634 Wilmslow Road, Didsbury, Manchester M20 3QX. E-mail: recruitment@teleca.com; Web: www.teleca.com	Manchester, Winchester, Swindon	
mainly applications developers and project management	1st	22	CV + letter	ongoing	Grazia Romano, Tenfold Systems UK Ltd, 18–20 Kew Road, Richmond, TW9 2NA. E-mail: gromano@tenfold.co.uk; Web: www.10fold.com	USA	

Page	Company	Type of business	Employees	Vacancies	Starting salary (£)	Benefits	Disciplines recruited from
	Tinsley Foods Ltd	chilled food processing	1,600	none in 2000	c 16k	pension scheme, 25 days' annual holiday, training programme	information technology, food technology, manufacturing, business studies
	Transco	gas distribution and transmission company	c. 15,000	c. 50	17,500–20,000	28 days' holiday; contributory pension, profit share scheme; free personal accident scheme etc.	engineering and commercial disciplines
	Triad Group plc	IT consultancy	350	10–20	20,000	life assurance; and after 6 months health insurance, pension	any
172	UBS Warburg	a broad-based investment bank	13,000 world	30	35k + 3k sign-on	full benefits including value-flex, medical insurance, pension plan etc..	computer science, management information, engineering, science, maths
	Unilever	FMCG	300,000	80	20,500	share-save scheme, pension, contributory health scheme	any
174	UNISYS	information services and technology	36,000 world	300	20,000+	healthcare plan, pension scheme, life assurance, 22 days' holiday, long-term disability, stock purchase plan	computer science/IT or related degrees, business or related degrees
	Vodafone	mobile telecommunications company	70,000+ world	c. 20	upper quartile	28 days' holiday, pension scheme, profit share, SAYE scheme, discounted products	computer science/studies, bus info systems, maths/stats, physics
	Xilinx	semiconductor	320	20	19K (punts)	stock options, pension, health insurance	engineering, IT, business
175	Yellow Pages	international directories and e-commerce business	5,000 UK and USA	2–3	17,000–19,500	financial assistance in relocation, bonus and contributory pension scheme	IT degree desirable
	Yorkshire Water	water management business	2,000	c. 20			any
	Zurich Financial Services	financial services	68,000	c. 20	20,000	flexible financial services benefits	any

Areas recruited to	Degree	UCAS points	How to apply	Closing date for applications	Contact	Other locations	BCS
IT, food technical, manufacturing, financial	2.2			Apply for details	The Recruitment Officer, Tinsley Foods Ltd, Sluice Road, Holbeach St. Marks, Spalding, Lincolnshire, PE12 8HF. Tel: 01406 702 221	none	✓
engineering and commercial roles	2.2		EAF	02/02/01	Julie McLaren, Transco Graduate Recruitment, c/o 42–43 West Street, Reading, Berks RG1 1TZ. Tel: 0118 952 0105; E-mail: julie.mclaren@pertemps.co.uk	nationwide	✓
	2.1		CV	N/A	Melanie Wilkinson, Recruitment and Training Manager, Triad Group plc, Weyside Park, Catteshall Lane, Godalming, Surrey GU7 1XE	any relevant client sites	
applications support/ developing tactical IT solutions/systems development	2.1		online	01/12/00	Web: www.ubswarburg.com	London, Conneticut, Chicago, Tokyo, Singapore, Hong Kong, Sydney, Zurich	
information management	3rd	6	online	12/01/01	Chris MacRae, Senior Recruitment Manager, Unilever House, Blackfriars, London EC4P 4BQ. Web: www.ucmds.com	around the UK	
information systems and technology consultants, software and hardware engineers, network consultants, programmers and systems analysts	2.1 or 2.2	16	online	ongoing	Graduate Recruitment Team, Bakers Court, Bakers Road, Uxbridge UB8 1RG. Web: www.unisysukgrads.com; Tel: 0800 917 9130	16 locations in the UK. Majority of vacancies in our Uxbridge, Slough, London, Glasgow and Milton Keynes offices	
varies	2.1	20	online, hotline 0700 267 7779	none	Tel: 0700 267 7779; Web: www.vodafone.co.uk/graduates	Newbury	
engineering, IT, business	2.2		CV + letter	30/11/00	Tel: +353 1 4640311; E-mail: xiradv@xilinx.com	Surrey, Edinburgh, Dublin	
all IT areas, including new media	2.2		CV + letter	16/02/01	Graduate Recruitment, Yellow Pages, Queens Walk, Reading RG1 7PT. E-mail: jobs@yellowpages.co.uk (subject: graduate)		
customer services, IT, finance, water and waste water business units	2.1		EAF	12/1/01	HR Service Centre, Western House, Western Way, Halifax Road, Bradford BD6 2LZ		
IT	2.1		post, e-mail, telephone	n/a	Maria Iacobaccio, Human Resources, Zurich Financial Services UK Life Ltd, Station Road, Swindon Road SN1 1EL. E-mail: maria.iacobaccio@zurich.co.uk; Tel: 01793 511 227; Fax: 01793 506 730	Swindon and Cheltenham	

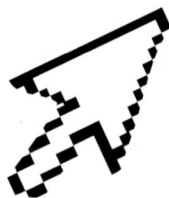

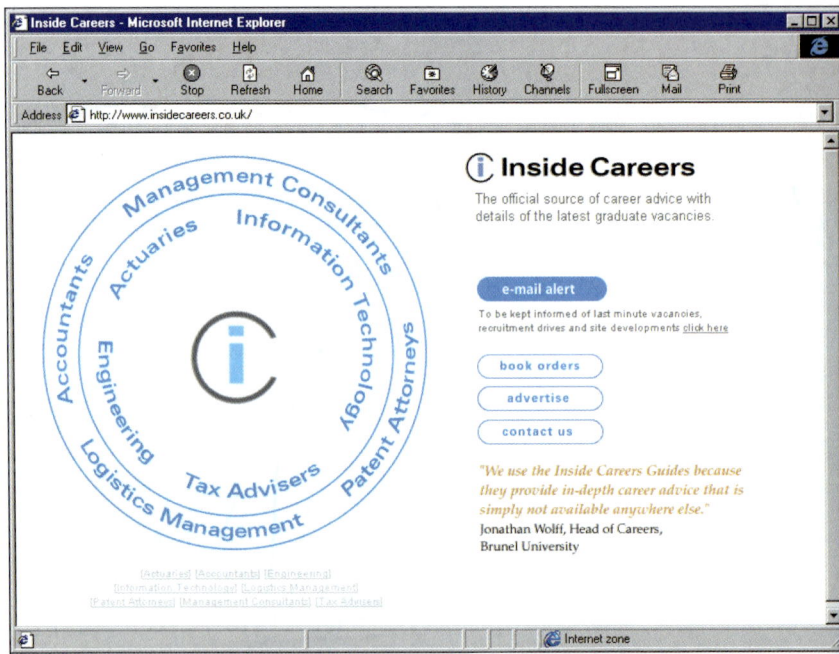